When Jesus Visits His Church

*A Study Of The Seven Churches of Asia
(Revelation Chapters 2-3)*

by R. Maurice Smith

© 2011, 2014 Copyright Rising River Media.
All rights reserved.

2014 Revised Edition

Written permission must be secured from the publisher to use or reproduce any part of this work in any form except where quotations are accompanied by a full and accurate recitation of the work's full title, the publisher, and the publisher's address. Additional copies of this publication are available from the addresses given below:

Published by Rising River Media, P.O. Box 9133, Spokane, WA 99209

Scripture quotations are from The Holy Bible, English Standard Version (ESV), Copyright 2001 by Crossway Bibles, a publishing ministry of Good News Publishers. Used by permission. All rights reserved.

www.risingrivermedia.org

Cover design & original art work by Gale A. Smith.
Cover photo and inside art licensed through istock.

ISBN 13   978-0-9960096-5-2

Table of Contents

Table of Contents 3

Author's Preface 5

Introduction 9
    "Behold, He Is Coming" 9
    Entering A Season of Divine Visitation 11
    Divine Visitations in the Old Testament 12
    Divine Visitations In The New Testament 13
    What Does This Mean For Us? 14
    Organic House Church And Revival 17

Setting The Stage For The Seven Churches 21
    When Did All This Take Place? 21
    Where Did All This Take Place? 22
    The Shared Christian Experience 23
    What Are The "Big Ideas"? 29
    Compromise - The Underlying Struggle 33
    General Format Of The Letters 34
    The Great Challenges 35

Ephesus 43
    The Letter 43
    Background of Ephesus 44
    Seven Observations 46
    When Jesus Visits Your House Church 59

Smyrna 63
    Then and Now 63
    Background of Smyrna 68
    When Jesus Visits Your House Church 75

Pergamum 79
    Background of Pergamum 79
    The Nicolaitans 83
    When Jesus Visits Your House Church 89

Thyatira 93
    Background of Thyatira 95
    Background Regarding "Jezebel" 99
    Five Lessons Regarding False Authority 102
    When Jesus Visits Your House Church 107

Sardis 111
    Background of Sardis 111
    A Lesson About Lamps, Oil And Power 112
    Five Commands 116
    When Jesus Visits Your House Church 121

Philadelphia 125
    The Opening and Closing of Doors 125
    Background of Philadelphia 126
    An Open Door 129
    When Jesus Visits Your House Church 135

Laodicea 139
    Background of Laodicea 140
    Your Apathy Makes Me Sick 142
    You Are Living A Delusion 143
    Let Me Give You Some Advice 145
    If I Didn't Love You, I Wouldn't Say This 146
    This Knock-Knock Is No Joke 148
    When Jesus Visits Your House Church 150

Epilogue 153
    A Time To Reflect 153
    The Challenge of Compromise 153
    The Biblical Antidote to Compromise 155
    Smyrna In Korea 156
    Are You A Compromised Church? 162
    A Prayer of Visitation 163

Author's Preface
To The Revised Edition

Through a variety of unforseen events the original print edition of this book never saw publication, although the electronic version was available as a Kindle book on Amazon. This revised edition has undergone numerous corrections and expansions from that original version, allowing the author to breathe a sigh of both thankfulness and relief that the original version saw such a limited circulation.

Let's begin this revised study together by asking a simple question: If Jesus were to visit your house church the same way He promised to visit the house churches in Asia Minor in Revelation Chapters 2 and 3, what would He find and what would He say?

Would He find faithfulness and perseverance in the face of persecution and the overwhelming pressures of maintaining a biblical witness in a hostile world? Would He find believers busy working much but loving little? Would He find believers so enamored with their "lampstand" (their church, their denomination, their ministry) that He must threaten to remove it? Would He find false teachers advocating scandalous indifference toward sin and idolatry? Would He find leaders and teachers exercising false authority and offering false teaching that leads God's people into compromise and sin? Would He find complacent believers living on their heritage and reputation? Would He find believers who have

When Jesus Visits His Church

compromised their faith with affluence and material prosperity? What would the Risen Christ find in your house church that would earn His blessing, or that would

> *"The problems faced by the Seven Churches of Asia are our problems today, and our issues were their issues."*

rightfully deserve His rebuke and admonition? And what would He find that could lead Him to say, "Change . . . or else!"? These are just a few of the issues and questions which the Risen Christ found among the Seven Churches of Asia as he prepared them for His upcoming visitation.

Very little has changed in the Church today. The problems faced by the Seven Churches of Asia are our problems today, and our issues were their issues. Times may change, but people, problems and issues don't. Not really. As we will see, all seven of the Churches of Asia were bound by a common, underlying threat - the threat of compromising their witness for Christ when faced with the challenges of an unbelieving hostile world. And one of the greatest challenges facing you, your house church and the Church of the 21st century is the pressure to compromise your witness before the eyes of a watching, skeptical and sometimes hostile world. Times may change, but the challenge of compromise remains the same. Only the circumstances are different.

This study arose out of my own personal study of revival and spiritual awakening - those seasons of divine visitation when God rends the heavens and comes down, seasons when

Jesus visits His Church to rebuke, to restore and to renew. I believe that the letters to the Seven Churches of Asia present us with numerous insights into what Jesus is looking for when He visits His Church. I believe we can use those insights as guides for how to seek God in preparation for a coming season of divine visitation and spiritual outpouring in revival. And it is for this purpose that I offer them for your consideration.

Maurice Smith
Rising River Media
Advent, 2014

When Jesus Visits His Church

Introduction

"Behold, He Is Coming"

"Behold, he is coming with the clouds, and every eye will see him, even those who pierced him, and all tribes of the earth will wail on account of him. Even so. Amen. 'I am the Alpha and the Omega,' says the Lord God, 'who is and who was and who is to come, the Almighty.'" (Rev 1:7-8)

We are all prisoners of our paradigms to some extent. We all find it very difficult to see life and reality in any terms other than those we have become accustomed to as taught to us by the terms of our paradigm. This includes how we see and understand Scripture - such as the book of Revelation. For example, The "Preterist" school of interpretation sees the book of Revelation as finding its fulfillment in the events leading up to AD 70 and the destruction of Jerusalem. On the other hand, the "Futurist" school of interpretation sees the book of Revelation as recording a yet-future history of events associated with the "end-times" just prior to Christ's return to earth. There are other schools of interpretation, but the end result is that the letters to the Seven Churches often get overlooked, ignored and absorbed into the larger debate of whether Revelation represents past history or predictive prophecy.[1] The tragedy for the contemporary church is that

---

[1] For a concise summary of the four (4) basic schools of interpretation, see George Eldon Ladd, ***A Commentary On The Revelation of John*** (Grand Rapids: William B. Eerdmans Publishing Company, 1972), page 10-12.

When Jesus Visits His Church

we have lost sight of the fact that Jesus is also speaking to His Church today through the same lessons which He imparted to the Seven Churches of 1st Century Asia.

For the duration of this book I want you to suspend your previous conceptions about the Seven Churches of Asia and think of them simply as seven house churches in seven cities in Asia Minor (Western Turkey) which had been planted

"You and I ARE the Church of Ephesus. You and I ARE the Church of Smyrna. You and I ARE the Seven Churches of Asia in Revelation 2-3. And Jesus has things He wants to say to us!"

and/or nurtured by apostolic leaders, but which had now fallen into decline and were in need of a divine visitation. Resist any temptation you might have to think of them as "epochs in Church history" (i.e., *"The Church in Sardis pictures the Reformation Church"* as one author declared). Instead, think of them as real Churches with real believers who were wrestling with real issues such as whether or not to compromise their faith when confronted with the demands of their surrounding communities. Think of them as real believers struggling with out-right persecution, false teachers, the "busy-ness" of ministry, complacency, sexual immorality, spiritual lukewarmness and other issues which are as real in the Church today as they were in the Church of A.D. 96 when John wrote. Think of them as real churches with real believers whom Jesus is warning that He is coming in a divine visitation to rebuke, to admonish, to correct, to

Introduction

encourage and to reward during a much-needed season of spiritual renewal and revival. Seen this way, as real churches filled with real people struggling with real issues, Jesus' words to them come alive as His words to us, too. You and I ARE the Church of Ephesus. You and I ARE the Church of Smyrna. You and I ARE the Seven Churches of Asia in Revelation 2-3. And Jesus has things He wants to say to us!

The goal of this study is to step out of any pre-conceived paradigms we might have brought with us and to ask the question, *"Is there a message here which is relevant to the Church today irrespective of any "end-time" debate?"* I believe the answer is "Yes!" There is a message here about preparing the people of God for a "divine visitation." Is there something in the lead-up to the seven letters that would suggest a "divine visitation"? Yes. In Revelation 1:7 the writer declares, *"Behold, He is coming . . ."* That's a pretty clear indication that a visitation is about to unfold.

Entering A Season of Divine Visitation

Every season of "revival" in the history of the Church has been a season of divine visitation. And what is about to unfold today is no exception. I believe that the Church of God is about to enter a season of divine visitation - a season of genuine spiritual "revival" or "awakening." I have written extensively about this in my book **Preparing For the Coming Spiritual Outpouring**. After several years of listening to God's voice regarding this coming season of visitation, certain things have become very clear to me. Most

When Jesus Visits His Church

important of these is that God desires an obedient *ekklesia* (Church) whose primary desire is to know Him and to seek Him in genuine humility, holiness and the fear of the Lord, and personal repentance. He desires an "agenda free" church, because God is His own agenda, and He is not willing to be used as the means to anyone else's end. And He desires a "holy" church that sets holiness, repentance and intimacy with Him as priorities above all else. To the extent that He is unable to find this among existing churches, paradigms and structures, He will go around existing structures and paradigms and raise up new ones. He has done this in previous revivals and outpourings, and He is doing it again today. God is calling His Church, His *ekklesia*, to a profound season of self examination, humility, holiness and the fear of the Lord, and personal repentance in preparation for a profound season of spiritual outpouring and divine visitation.[2]

Divine Visitations in the Old Testament

Scripture actually has a lot to say about divine visitations. The Hebrew concept of "visitation" comes from the Hebrew root *pqd* (*paqad*). The root meaning is *"to seek out, to visit, to see to someone or something,"* hence, *"to seek attentively or in an examining manner to someone or something."* It is a term which describes God's "beneficial attention" toward His

---

[2] See our book, ***The Inextinguishable Blaze: God's Call To Holiness, Repentance, Intimacy And Spiritual Awakening***, available through our website from Amazon.com.

Introduction

people.

In the writings of the Old Testament prophets, God's visitation takes on the sense of God coming to visit in

> *"God's visitations are a two-edged sword - they can bless, or they can hold people accountable in judgment."*

order to examine and to call people to accountability and responsibility (not unlike what we will see among the Seven Churches of Asia in Revelation). Of the 300+ occurrences of the word in the Old Testament, 86 occur in the Prophetic books, and 49 of those 86 occur in the Book of Jeremiah. A significant aspect of Jeremiah's ministry was preparing God's people for a coming visitation, and what such a visitation might mean. We can see a typical use of the word *pqd* by Jeremiah in this verse, *"Shall I not punish (visit) these people, declares the Lord, and on a nation such as this shall I not avenge Myself."* (Jeremiah 5:9; 5:29 and 9:9). Here, God's visitation is construed by the translators of the NASB in terms of judgment or punishment. This raises an important point: How God's visitation is to be interpreted depends upon the context. God's visitations are a two-edged sword - they can bless, or they can hold people accountable in judgment.

Divine Visitations In The New Testament

In the New Testament the Greek word for visitation is *episkope* from the Greek verb *episkeptomai*, meaning *"to*

When Jesus Visits His Church

look upon, to consider, to have regard to, something or someone." It is the word used most commonly by the Greek Old Testament (the Septuagint) to translate the Hebrew pqd, thereby linking the O.T. concept with the New Testament writers. In the N.T. this visitation takes place *"when God draws near to His people in its sin and distress, and shows Himself to be the Lord of History. It may entail the judgment executed by Him. But it may also consist in an act of mercy. The point is that He manifestly enters history. The word "to visit" may signify a visitation of both judgment and grace in the same sentence."* We will see this two-edged principle regarding God's visitation illustrated in the Seven Churches of Asia. The Risen Christ comes with a message of both blessing (for obedience) and judgment (for continued disobedience). That's the nature of God's visitations. They are a two-edged sword that both blesses and judges.

> *"That's the nature of God's visitations. They are a two-edged sword that both blesses and judges."*

What Does This Mean For Us?

So, what does all of this mean for us and for the possibility of spiritual revival? **First,** I believe the messages of the Risen Christ to the Seven Churches of Asia are also messages to His Church today. Their story is our story; and our story was their story. The same problems which existed in those Churches two thousand years ago also exist today. And in

Introduction

the coming visitation of revival, the Risen Christ intends to confront us with the same challenges, warnings and solutions as He presented to them.

Second, as one who has been intimately involved with the organic house church movement over the past 15 years, I think it is note-worthy that these messages of the Risen Christ were directed to house

> *". . . every season of revival represents a visitation from God; and every season of judgment represents a visitation from God. The same God does both. And sometimes he even does both simultaneously."*

churches meeting in the homes of believers in each of these cities. This had been the pattern throughout the New Testament, and would continue to be for the next 200 or so years, until the reign of the Emperor Constantine in the early 300s A.D. Simply put, their context (house churches) is our context, and our context was their context. Remember that.

Third, every season of revival represents a visitation from God; and every season of judgment represents a visitation from God. The same God does both. And sometimes he even does both simultaneously. The divine visitation promised to the Seven Churches of Asia was a visitation that would bring either spiritual renewal or judgment, depending upon their response to His warnings and admonitions.

This idea of a two-edged visitation bringing both revival and

When Jesus Visits His Church

judgment can be found in the Old Testament book of Jeremiah and the great revival under King Josiah, perhaps the greatest revival in the history of the southern Kingdom of Judah. It is a breathtaking story of seeking God on both a personal and a national scale. But equally breathtaking is the fact that Jeremiah began his prophetic ministry in the 13th year of King Josiah's reign. The first ten chapters of Jeremiah cover the 18 years of reform and revival under Josiah. It is in those first 10 chapters of Jeremiah that we see God declaring three times: *"Shall I not punish (visit) these people, declares the Lord, and on a nation such as this shall I not avenge Myself."* The reformation and revival under Josiah was like a river which flowed a mile wide, but only an inch deep.

I believe that we are indeed entering into a new season of God's Visitation. God is about to pay His church a visit.

"The reformation and revival under Josiah was like a river which flowed a mile wide, but only an inch deep."

We assume that such a visit will be a season of great blessing. I, too, believe that to be true. But that is only half of the story of what it means when God pays a visit. The up-coming visitation may occur during a season in which God calls His church into accountability; to say nothing of the possibility that He may well call the unbelieving world into accountability for such things as abortion, homosexuality, rampant sexual immorality, abuse of the poor and down-trodden, and much more. This is why I believe it is

Introduction

imperative that we as the Church and as the house church movement embrace this unfolding season of God's visitation with earnest humility through personal and corporate prayer and fasting and repentance; so that when this season is done, the same terrible words are not pronounced against us as were pronounced against the religious people of Jesus' day, *"thou knewest not the time (<u>kairos</u> - season) of thy visitation."*

Organic House Church And Revival

There is much talk today about both revival and house church. Much of the revival talk that I have heard, and much of the activity I have seen, resembles men attempting to organize a parade complete with food, music and entertainment in the hope that God will show up and agree to lead it. I confess that there have been times that I, too, have engaged in the same behavior. But is that really God's heart? And is that really what we want God to do? Is that what we are praying and longing for in terms of spiritual outpouring and revival? Or are we willing to invite God to *"rend the heavens and come down"* and to send the Holy Spirit on His terms, even if the price of such a visitation includes our own profound "death-to-self"? Parades are fun - death to self is not.

And what does all of this have to do with house church? Bill Beckham, an internationally recognized leader in the cell church movement, makes a profound observation when he observes, *"You never change a structure until you change a*

When Jesus Visits His Church

value. We do not transplant systems and structures. We transplant values and life." Amen! Much of what I have observed and experienced in the organic house church movement thus far, including the current rising interest in house church among traditional church practitioners, represents a *"fiddling with the structure,"* an experimentation with methodology, rather than a genuine imbibing and incarnation of new values - new wine skins sans the requisite new wine. This cannot and will not last. Infatuation with the "novel" never does.

When we look at the house-to-house pattern of church in Acts 2:41-47 I am reminded that it was the product of Acts 2:1-40 and the Pentecostal outpouring of the Holy Spirit that brought thousands to new-found faith in Christ.

> *"If we are not careful, 'organic house church' will become little more than a new structure in search of a value, a wine skin in search of wine."*

The new wine of Acts 2:1-40 produced the new wine skins of Acts 2:41-47. That's the way it works. Not the other way around. If we are not careful, "organic house church" will become little more than a new structure in search of a value, a wine skin in search of wine. And that would be disastrous.

But I believe that God has different plans. I believe we are standing on the eve of an outpouring of the River of Ezekiel 47 the like of which has not been seen or experienced in well over 100 years. And like those early believers of Acts

Introduction

Chapter 2, this is the "value" that will create, fill and guide our structure throughout this generation, and probably well into the next. But I believe that the Spirit of God would ask you the same question which He has asked me: *"Is this what you seek? Is this the outpouring you desire? Are you prepared to welcome me on my terms?"* Are you? Are you prepared to embrace the profound "death-to-self" that it may (and probably will) require? Are you prepared for your house church to become a new channel through which the River of His Spirit can flow? When the values of our house church "structure" are examined by future generations, let it be said of us, *"They set their hearts to become a channel through which the River of God could flow . . . and He did."*

What are you doing to prepare for this coming season of divine visitation? That was the ultimate question facing those early believers in the Seven Churches of Asia, and it is the question facing us as believers today as we seek God in prayer and fasting, asking Him to visit us by sending the River of His Spirit to flow through us and our house churches in revival and spiritual awakening.

He is coming. Are you ready?

When Jesus Visits His Church

Setting The Stage For The Seven Churches

"I, John, your brother and partner in the tribulation and the kingdom and the patient endurance that are in Jesus, was on the island called Patmos on account of the word of God and the testimony of Jesus." (Rev 1:9)

When Did All This Take Place?

The generally accepted view of Revelation is that it was written by John, the Son of Zebedee, the beloved disciple of Jesus who also wrote the Gospel and Letters of John. Although some have argued for an earlier date in the late 50s or early 60s AD, the evidence is strong that John wrote Revelation in the last decade of the 1st Century, toward the end of the reign of the Emperor Domitian who came to the Imperial Throne of Rome in A.D.81. Whereas previous Emperors had allowed themselves to be worshiped during their lifetimes and to be deified by the Senate following their deaths, Domitian was the first of the emperors to assume the status of "god," claiming the title of <u>Dominus et Deus</u> ("Lord and God") while he was still alive. The Church Historian Eusebius of Caesarea says that the Emperor Domitian *"Established himself as the successor of Nero (AD 54-67), in his hatred and hostility to God. He was the second that raised a persecution against us . . . ."* Eusebius goes on to quote the testimony of Hegesippus who reported that John returned to Ephesus, from which he had been banished and exiled to the penal island of Patmos by the Emperor

When Jesus Visits His Church

Domitian, upon being released from exile after the ascension of Nerva to the Imperial Throne in A.D. 96. This would give us a "rough date" of A.D. 96 for the book of Revelation and the letters to the Seven Churches of Asia.[3]

It is worth a brief note here to observe how quickly good churches can decline to the point of needing a divine visitation to "straighten out" what is wrong. The Apostle Paul had spent some three years ministering in Ephesus and the surrounding area during his third missionary journey (See Acts 19) in roughly A.D. 57-60. According to Church tradition, Paul's ministry in Ephesus was followed by the ministry of the Apostle John, probably up until his exile by the Emperor Domitian in the early A.D. 80s. Yet, within only a few years (by A.D. 96) Ephesus and the surrounding Churches had fallen into serious decline - so serious that the Risen Christ had to threaten personal intervention in order to address what was wrong. This should be a warning to ALL of us concerning the need for ongoing vigilance to avoid that same precipitous spiritual decline in our own lives and ministries.

Where Did All This Take Place?

The Roman Province of Asia, where all Seven Churches were located, encompassed the western and southwestern portions of Asia Minor, what the ancient Greeks called "Anatolia" (modern Western Turkey). The local

---

[3]Ladd, ***A Commentary On The Revelation Of John***, page 7.

Background

religious/social culture was idolatrous, polytheistic and riddled with ritual religious prostitution, making it naturally hostile to the anti-idolatry, monotheistic("One God") and moral teaching of Christianity. Add to this the local commitment to the Imperial Cult of Roman Emperor Worship and the stage was set for both conflict and compromise. As Paul discovered during his prolonged ministry in Ephesus (See Acts Chapter 19), the proclamation of the Gospel has a dramatic impact upon such a culture. Under Paul's ministry the gospel refuted and quenched magic and witchcraft, causing the local residents to burn their magic books and to withdraw from participation in the local temple cult of worship to the goddess Diana (Artemis). This, in turn, had a dramatic impact upon the trade in silver idols, irritating the local silversmiths, inciting a riot and threatening the existing political structure. It is likely that the spread of the gospel had no less of an impact upon the six other cities in Asia which received letters from the Risen Christ.

The Shared Christian Experience

"I, John, your brother and fellow partaker in the tribulation and kingdom and perseverance which are in Jesus . . ." (1:9)

According to the Apostle John, as believers we share three things by virtue of the fact that we are "in Jesus": [4]

---

[4]Greek: *sugkoinonos* - *"something held in common together,"* hence, *"co-partaker"*

When Jesus Visits His Church

We Share In A "tribulation" - According to John we share in "the tribulation" which is "in Jesus." The Greek word translated "tribulation" (*thlipsis* - "pressure") occurs 45 times in 43 verses in the New Testament. Its root meaning is *"to crush, press or squeeze."* The idea is *"the pressure of crushing distress."* Ladd explains the origin of this "pressure of crushing distress" when he says,

"Back of human history are mighty spiritual powers in conflict with each other - the Kingdom of God and the power of Satan. The church stands between the two. The church is th people to whom the Kingdom has come and who will inherit the Kingdom when it comes; but as such, it is the object of satanic hatred and is destined to suffer tribulation. Tribulation here includes all the evil which will befall the church, but especially the great tribulation at the end, which will be only the intensification of what the church has suffered throughout all history." [5]

The concept of tribulation is a frequent idea in the New Testament:

1. It is used to describe end-time distress (Matthew 24:9, 21, 29)
2. It is used to describe child-birth (John 16:21)
3. Jesus promised that we would have tribulation in this world (John 16:33)
4. It is used to describe the persecution of the Church

---

[5]Ladd, page 30.

Background

     after the stoning of Stephen (Acts 11:9)
5. Tribulation is part of our journey into the Kingdom of God (Acts 14:22)
6. The Holy Spirit told Paul that tribulation would accompany his ministry (Acts 20:33)
7. The purpose of tribulation is to produce perseverance (see below) in us (Romans 5:3)
8. One of the characteristics of the Christian life is persevering in tribulation (Romans 12:12)
9. Paul experienced tribulation in Asia that caused him to despair even of life (2 Corinthians 1:8)
10. Two characteristics of "servants" in ministry are "perseverance" and "tribulation" (2 Corinthians 6:4)

Even though our sharing in *"the pressure of crushing distress"* is something promised by Jesus, experienced by the early Church and taught as a character-building quality of the Christian life, such

"If tribulation is the lot and promise of God's people in this present evil age (and it is), then the Kingdom is the lot and promise of God's people in the Age to Come."

tribulation is not a very popular topic among believers today. It just doesn't seem to fit well with the popular notion of enjoying *"your best life now."* What kind of tribulation - what pressure of crushing distress - is God allowing in your life right now? And what is it producing in you?

We Share In A "Kingdom" - According to John we also

When Jesus Visits His Church

share in "the Kingdom " which is "in Jesus." If tribulation is the lot and promise of God's people in this present evil age, then the Kingdom is the lot and promise of God's people in the Age to Come.

The Greek word *basileia* appears 34 times from Acts to Revelation with reference to the Kingdom of God.

1. The Kingdom of God was the message of both John the Baptist and Jesus (Matthew 3:2; 4:17; Mark 1:15)
2. We enter the Kingdom of God through a new birth (John 3:3)
3. God has chosen to freely give us the Kingdom (Luke 12:32)
4. It is not yet of this world (John 18:36)
5. It is the future inheritance of the righteous (1 Corinth.6:9-10; 15:24 and 50; Galatians 5:21; Ephesians 5:5; James 2:5)
6. The Kingdom of God was an integral part of the preaching of the early Church (Acts 8:12; 14:22; 19:8; 20:25; 28:23)
7. Nowhere in the New Testament are believers ever called "kings." But believers are called "servants" (Greek: *doulos* - "bond-servant") no less than two dozen times.
8. We are a "kingdom of priests" (Revelation 1:6; 5:10) called not to rule in this present evil age, but to worship. With respect to God, we are priests; with respect to men we are servants.

Background

What do you know and understand about this "kingdom" of which you are a fellow-partaker with believers throughout the ages? Do you understand your place and role in it? How are you now fulfilling the two roles of believers in the Kingdom of God: How are you a "priest" in this Kingdom who worships God and who teaches others to do the same? How are you a "servant" in this Kingdom who serves others?

We Share In A "patient endurance" - Finally, according to John, we share in "the patient endurance" which is "in Jesus." The Greek word *hupomone* literally means *"to abide under,"* or *"patient waiting under pressure."* In other words, "perseverance." Of the seven times this word occurs in the book of Revelation, four of them

"Perseverance assumes tribulation, and tribulation requires and produces perseverance."

are found in Chapters 2-3, and one more is found in the introduction to the letters (1:9). Perseverance refers to that quality of patient endurance that does not surrender to circumstances or succumb under trial. It is *"patience under pressure."* Barclay describes perseverance as *"courageous galantry which accepts suffering and hardship and loss and turns them into grace and glory."* [6]

In the New Testament perseverance is an important

---

[6]William Barclay, ***The Revelation of John***, Volume 1, Revised Edition (Philadelphia: The Westminster Press, 1976), page 62.

When Jesus Visits His Church

character quality of the Christian life, only produced by tribulation. Perseverance assumes tribulation, and tribulation requires and produces perseverance. Here are a few of the things the New Testament has to say about "perseverance":

1. In Romans 8: 25 and 1 Thessalonians 1:3 Paul relates perseverance to "hope." Genuine biblical hope embodies a favorable and confident expectation of good from God in the face of tribulation. We persevere under the pressure of crushing distress because of the favorable and confident expectation we have in the goodness of God and the ultimate triumph of His Kingdom.
2. Paul reminded his young disciple Timothy that perseverance was one of the characteristics which Timothy had witnessed in Paul's own ministry (2 Timothy 3:10).
3. The writer of Hebrews reminds his readers that they are engaged in a race which requires perseverance to run successfully (Hebrews 12:1).
4. James reminds his readers of the perseverance of Job as an example to follow (James 5:11).

As demonstrated among the Seven Church of Asia, the early Church understood the importance of tribulation and perseverance in the life of the individual believer as well as in the corporate life of the church. How is God using the *"the pressure of crushing distress"* (tribulation) to work perseverance into your life?

Background

What Are The "Big Ideas"?

Each of the Seven Churches of Asia had their unique situation which set them apart from one another, but they all shared some things in common. This is why their messages are both local and universal. These *"lessons held in common"* represent what I refer to as the "Big Ideas." And it is the vocabulary of the letters which helps us to identify some of these "Big Ideas."

"Deeds" (Greek: _ergon_): This is the general Greek term for "work" or "deeds" and is used 13 times in 5 letters, but does not appear at all in 2 of them. The "Big Idea" is simple: Jesus knows our deeds, our works, both good and bad. What we discover in these letters is that, although good deeds are important, good deeds are never enough by themselves. It is never enough to simply work hard for Jesus.[7]

"Repent" (Greek: _metanoia_): This is the most frequent command found in the 7 letters, used 8 times in 5 letters, but not in two others (Smyrna and Philadelphia). The "Big Idea" here is simple and profound: Repentance is God's prescribed medicine for bringing a wandering church (or individual believer) back into obedience to God's will and purposes. Unfortunately, repentance is the lost heart of the Church

---

[7]This is not to minimize the importance of good deeds in the life of the believer. See our book, ***The Least Of These: The Role Of Good Deeds In A Jesus-Shaped Spirituality***, available through our website from Amazon.

When Jesus Visits His Church

today, which makes the message of the Seven Churches of Asia all the more relevant to us today.

"Overcome" (Greek: <u>nikao</u>): Each of the Seven Churches is challenged by the Risen Christ to "conquer" or "overcome." The term is used 7 times in 7 letters. The "Big Idea" is that the Christian life, both individually and corporately, is a journey on which we are called to conquer or overcome the obstacles and challenges placed before us by the world, the flesh and the devil. But it is important to note: Christians are not automatically assumed to be conquerors or overcomers; rather, we are called and challenged to become conquerors and overcomers. Overcoming requires intentionality and effort on our part.

> *"Christians are not automatically assumed to be conquerors or overcomers; rather, we are called and challenged to become conquerors and overcomers."*

"Listen Up" (Greek: <u>akouo</u>): Each of the Seven Letters contains an admonition to "listen up." The word appears 7 times in 7 letters, always in the aorist subjunctive, *"He who has an ear,* **let him hear** *what the Spirit says to the churches."*[8] Again, the "Big Idea" is simple and clear: We

---

[8] Use of the Aorist Subjunctive suggests simple "contingent" action expressing a degree of doubt as to the outcome. In other words, it remained an open question as to whether or not the churches would listen.

Background

need to listen carefully to what the Spirit is saying to the each of the Seven Churches. Why? Because Jesus' word to each of them is His word to us, too. Because we ARE the Church of Ephesus, and the Church of Smyrna, and the Church of Pergamum, and the Church of Thyatira, and the Church of Sardis, and the Church of Philadelphia, and the Church of Laodicea. We ARE the Seven Churches of Asia. The only question is, *"Which Church are you today?"*

There are other "Big Ideas" which will come to light as we examine each of the seven letters, but these will help us to set the tone of the letters and to understand the urgency of their message for us today.

The Churches And Their Issues

It is easy for anyone trying to understand and come to terms with the Seven Churches to get lost in all of the churches, images and messages. In order to help clear the air and to identify the message of each church, I have prepared the summary chart on the following page. I hope it will help you to identify each church, its challenge and its message.

When Jesus Visits His Church

A Summary of The Churches And Their Challenge		
The Church	*The Issue*	*The Challenge*
Ephesus	***Love:*** They had left their first love	***Repent!*** Return to faith and love.
Smyrna	***Fear:*** Don't fear what's coming	"Be faithful unto death"
Pergamum	***Idolatry:*** False teachers advocating compromise toward idolatry & Emperor Worship	***Repent!*** Or I will come and make war with you!
Thyatira	***Immorality:*** Tolerating false teachers who advocate compromise and sexual immorality	***Repent!*** "Hold fast what you have."
Sardis	***Complacency:*** Spiritually dead and living on their reputation	***Repent!*** Remember and wake up!
Philadelphia	***Faithfulness:*** You haven't denied my name!	"Hold fast to what you have"
Laodicea	***Affluence:*** Affluence had led to a Lukewarm faith	***Repent!*** And be zealous.

Background

Compromise - The Underlying Struggle

When we view the Seven Churches as a group we quickly realize that these churches shared a common struggle, namely, the temptation to compromise their faith.

Compromise In The Seven Churches of Asia	
The Church	*The Compromise*
Ephesus	Compromised their love for God and others by substituting good works and sound doctrine.
Smyrna	Resisted and avoided compromise by choosing faithfulness in face of persecution and death
Pergamum	Compromised by embracing false teachers (Nicolaitans) who advocated "scandalous indifference" toward idolatry (Emperor Worship).
Thyatira	Compromised by accepting the false authority of false teachers (Jezebel) who advocated indulgence in sexual immorality
Sardis	Compromised with complacency by living on their reputation
Philadelphia	Resisted compromise by exercising perseverance and faithfulness in the face of persecution
Laodicea	Compromised their faith with affluence.

When Jesus Visits His Church

Merriam-Webster defines "compromise" as *"a concession to something derogatory or prejudicial (eg. a compromise of principles)."* Each of the Seven Churches of Asia were engaged in an ongoing struggle with the

"Compromise with our surrounding culture remains one of the greatest threats to the witness and power of the Church, both then and now."

ever-present temptation to compromise their faith by making spiritual and moral concessions to their circumstances. The Risen Christ was well aware of these temptations and warned His Churches against both the dangers and the consequences of compromise. Very little has changed today. Compromise with our surrounding culture remains one of the greatest threats to the witness and power of the Church, both then and now.

When Jesus visits His Church in the upcoming visitation in revival and spiritual outpouring, what kind of compromise will He find in your life and in the life of your house church?

Remember: *In the Kingdom of God, there is no prize for those who spiritually and morally compromise.*

General Format Of The Letters

There is a general pattern or structure (with occasional exceptions) to the seven letters. The structure serves to let us know that there is a consistency to Jesus' dealings with

Background

His people, and yet the variations are sufficient to assure us that Jesus treats people and churches as individuals. The pattern runs as follows:

The Structure Of The Seven Letters	
Introduction	*"Here's Who I am In Relation To You"*
Acknowledgment/ Praise	*"Here's What I Know About What You've Been Doing"*
Confrontation	*"Here's The Issue I Have With You"*
Admonition	*"Here's What You Need To Do - Or Else"*
Additional Comment	*"Here's Something Else That I Noticed About You"*
Exhortation	*"Listen up! Do You Hear What I'm Saying To You?"*
Reward	*"Just Between You and Me"*

The Great Challenges Of The 1st Century

The early Church of the 1st Century faced three great challenges which are clearly reflected in the book of Revelation.

When Jesus Visits His Church

The Challenge Of Emperor Worship (State/Civil Religion)
- The Roman Emperor Nero (AD 54-68) was the first Roman Emperor to systematically persecute Christians, using them as scapegoats for the burning of Rome in July of AD 64. From the time of Nero for the next 250 years Christianity was an illegal religion, the profession and practice of which was punishable by death. People accused before Roman Magistrates of being Christians were given the opportunity to recant and offer a pinch of incense at a shrine to the Emperor while declaring "Caesar is Lord." Those who refused were executed. This practice has been thoroughly documented through correspondence between the Emperor Trajan and Pliny, the Governor of Bythinia in Asia Minor, dating from AD 117.[9]

In more recent times, Korean Missionary William Blair ("Gold In Korea") documented similar events in Korea during the 1930s leading up to the 2nd World War."[10] Japan, which had ruled Korea since the Sino-Russian War of the early 1900s, began installing shrines to the Japanese Emperor in public places and forcing the Korean people to visit the shrines in order to "honor" the Emperor. It was primarily the Christian Church in Korea which resisted this movement (at great cost and persecution) and encouraged Christians not to

---

[9] Pliny the Younger, *Letters* 10.96-97. Available on line at - http://faculty.georgetown.edu/jod/texts/pliny.html

[10] William Newton Blair, ***Gold In Korea***. Available through the Central Distributing Department of the Presbyterian Church (USA). 3rd edition (1957).

Background

participate. As Blair observed, *"Christianity gives men backbone"* (more about this when we examine the Church of Smyrna).

The Challenge Of Pagan Culture. Genuine Christianity has always come to eventual blows with authoritarianism on the one hand (the Roman Government), and moral anarchy on the other (the Roman Culture). In the 1st Century Churches of Asia, this challenge and this conflict can be seen in the pressure for Christians to engage in pagan social practices which involved sexual compromise and immorality. The present-day pressure upon the Church to compromise on the issue of homosexuality and same-sex marriage is simply the latest manifestation of this cultural pressure to endorse and/or engage in pagan social practices which involve sexual compromise and immorality. In this very real sense, we ARE the Church of Thyatira.

Judaizers and False Religion - Throughout the first century there was a growing antagonism and separation between the Church on the one hand, and Judaism and the Synagogue on the other. The distinctive teaching of the New Testament was (and is) that the true people of God are determined by grace, not by race. The true people of God are known by their relationship to Jesus, not by their genealogy. The Kingdom of God consists of people of every race, tribe and tongue who have become a single people of God through faith in Jesus Christ and who now share a common single root (Romans 11:16-24).

When Jesus Visits His Church

Beginning in Acts 15, the Christian insistence upon the doctrine of justification by faith apart from works of the Old Testament Law slowly drove a wedge between *ekklesia* and synagogue. Jewish teachers who insisted that keeping the "Laws of Moses" was necessary in addition to faith in Jesus for salvation came to be known as "Judaizers."

By the fall of Jerusalem in AD 70, the Church and the Synagogue had clearly moved in two different directions with strong antipathy between the two. In approximately AD 90, the re-constituted Jewish Sanhedrin re-worded one of the blessings recited daily in the synagogues so as to make it impossible for 'Nazarenes' (Jewish Christians) to take part in synagogue worship. This blessing, which traditionally included a curse on the enemies of God, was revised so that the curse said, *"let Nazarenes and heretics perish as in a moment; let them be blotted out of the book of life and not be enrolled with the righteous."* [11] The revision was approved by the Sanhedrin and adopted in the synagogues, so that "Nazarenes" (i.e., Jewish Christians) by keeping silent when the words were recited by the congregation, would give themselves away.

This open hostility between the Church and the Synagogue is clearly reflected in the letters of the Risen Christ to the Churches of Smyrna (Rev 2:9) and Philadelphia (Rev 3:9)

---

[11] F.F. Bruce, ***The Gospel of John*** (Grand Rapids: William B. Eerdmans Publishing Company, 1993), p. 215. Bruce's footnotes on this point are extensive.

Background

where the Risen Christ refers to the local Jewish communities as a "synagogue of Satan."

Let's Summarize

Before we move on to the Letters and the Churches themselves, and at the risk of being a little redundant, let's take a moment to summarize where we've been.

The Seven Churches Of Asia represent real people and real churches, struggling with real issues in the late 1st Century AD, not future ages, periods or epochs in church history. Their issues are our issues. The times and the circumstance may have changed for us, but the root issue remains the same: the temptation to compromise our faith with the values of our surrounding culture. For this reason alone, we need to listen carefully to what the Spirit is saying to the each of the Seven Churches. Why? Because Jesus' words to each of them are His word to us, too.

When Jesus Visits His Church

Ephesus
(Revelation 2:1-7)

(1) "To the angel of the church in Ephesus write: 'The words of him who holds the seven stars in his right hand, who walks among the seven golden lampstands. (2) I know your works, your toil and your patient endurance, and how you cannot bear with those who are evil, but have tested those who call themselves apostles and are not, and found them to be false. (3) I know you are enduring patiently and bearing up for my name's sake, and you have not grown weary. (4) But I have this against you, that you have abandoned the love you had at first. (5) Remember therefore from where you have fallen; repent, and do the works you did at first. If not, I will come to you and remove your lampstand from its place, unless you repent. (6) Yet this you have: you hate the works of the Nicolaitans, which I also hate. (7) He who has an ear, let him hear what the Spirit says to the churches. To the one who conquers I will grant to eat of the tree of life, which is in the paradise of God.'"

When Jesus Visits His Church

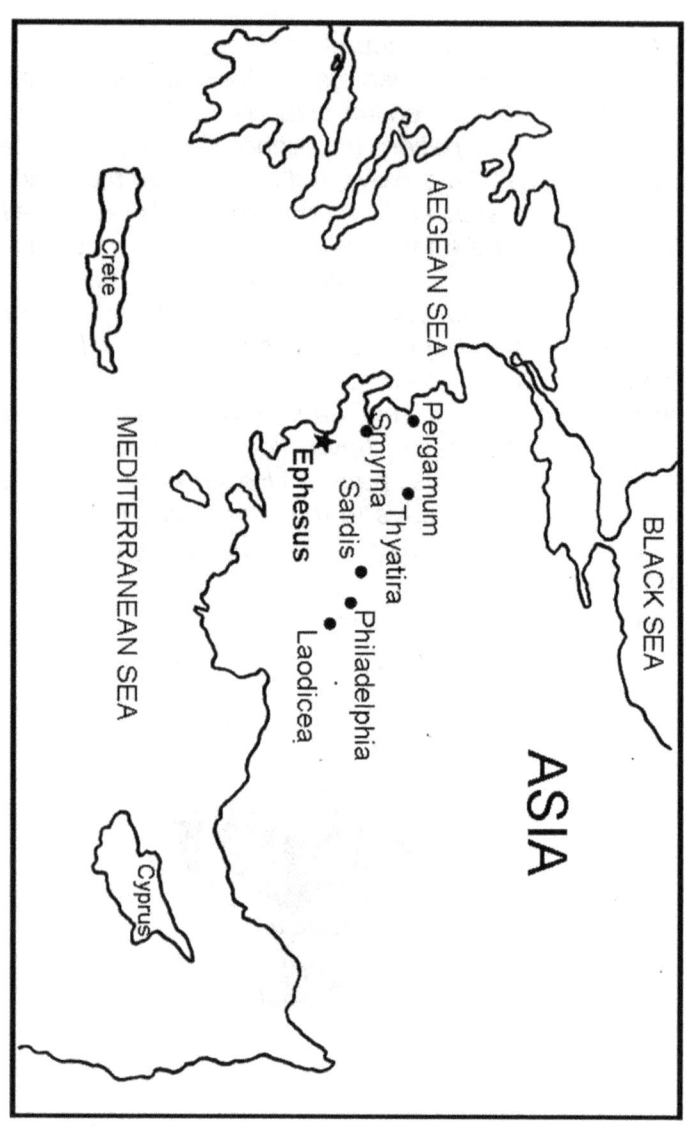

Ephesus
*The Church That Replaced
Intimacy With Work
(Revelation 2:1-7)*

The Letter

Consider this possible scene. It's Sunday morning. You're the pastor of a seemingly successful and growing church. You've been working hard with great toil and perseverance. And now the programs you have labored over are running smoothly, people are responding, the church looks healthy, even growing. Just prior to the morning service (or services!) a messenger arrives with a letter addressed to you and your church. You open it (Where did that messenger go? He seemed to just disappear?!) and to your amazement it is a letter for you and your church, and the sender is none other than the Lord Jesus Himself! Here is what He writes: *"Dear Pastor and Church, I know your works, your toil and your patient endurance, and how you cannot bear with those who are evil, but have tested those who call themselves apostles and are not, and found them to be false. (3) I know you are enduring patiently and bearing up for my name's sake, and you have not grown weary.* Your heart leaps within you. Yes! Finally! The Lord has noticed what we have done here and He is pleased! With great restraint you resist an almost overwhelming urge to do a quick "victory dance"!

But there is more to the letter, so you read on. And then it hits you. The words leap out at you from the page. Your short-lived joy suddenly turns to astonishment as you read,

When Jesus Visits His Church

"But I have this against you, that you have abandoned the love you had at first."

Left our first love; how could He possibly say that?! We've poured our heart and our soul into the ministry of this church (or organization). Doesn't He see? Attendance is up! Giving is up! False teachers are being regularly refuted and skewered! We've become a purpose driven church for heaven's sake! Doesn't He understand how well things are going?

What does He mean when He says, *"Remember therefore from where you have fallen."* I didn't know we had fallen! We aren't falling, we're growing! And what does He mean by "repent"? What are we supposed to repent for? And what's this *"remove your lampstand"* business? It sounds like I just got voted off the island in some "Church Survivor" episode and now somebody is going to snuff out my torch!

Now you know how the leadership of the Church at Ephesus must have felt when they received this very letter from the Apostle John in Revelation 2:1-7. History records that the Church at Ephesus never did repent, and the Church there eventually died out along with the city, both of which are now uninhabited ruins. And therein lies a story of a Church that replaced intimacy with work.

Background of Ephesus

Ephesus was situated on the coast of Asia Minor some 60

Ephesus

miles northeast of the Isle of Patmos where John received the Revelation. Ephesus ranked first in importance among the Seven Churches of Asia. As Ladd observes, *"Ephesus was both the foremost city of Asia and the home of the most important church in the province."* [12] In ancient times Ephesus was a strategically important city. Along with Rome, Antioch and Alexandria, Ephesus was one of the four greatest cities of the Roman Mediterranean world. Trade routes led there, and merchant ships sailed to and from its great harbor at the mouth of the Cayster River. But by New Testament times Ephesus was a city in decline. Its famous harbor suffered from silting and the city was slowly being by-passed by the major movements of trade. But as its coinage showed, it was still "The Landing Place," the port at which the Roman proconsul of Asia landed and where he had his official seat. And it was home to one of the seven wonders of the ancient world - the great Artemision - the magnificent temple to the goddess Artemis (Diana), which according to ancient reports was four times the size of Athens' Parthenon. With a first-century population of nearly 250,000 people it was the brightest of the "golden lampstands."

The Church at Ephesus had begun under the ministry of the Apostle Paul and two Jewish-Christian exiles from Rome (Acts 18:2), named Aquila and Priscilla. They had come with Paul from Corinth, and apparently stayed behind in Ephesus when Paul left for Antioch. Later, Paul returned to Ephesus and spent between two and three years there on his third

---

[12]Ladd, ***A Commentary On The Revelation Of John***, page 37.

When Jesus Visits His Church

missionary journey (Acts 19:9) with the result that *"all who lived in Asia heard the word of the Lord, both Jews and Greeks."* (Acts 19:10) It was Paul's preaching against idolatry in Ephesus that had resulted in a riot among the silversmiths who made their living making statues of Artemis. Later, church history and tradition hold that the Apostle John resided there as Bishop of Ephesus.

Seven Observations

Now, in order to tell this story without getting lost in its details, I want to make a series of "Observations" and then elaborate on them.

<u>*'Here's Who I Am In Relation To You'*</u>[13]

To the angel of the church in Ephesus write: The One who holds the seven stars in His right hand, the One who walks among the seven golden lampstands, says this: (2:1)

Observation # 1: *Jesus knows our situation, and always comes to us in a way that is unique to us.* Ephesus was a church with a rich apostolic history. We're talking serious apostolic pedigree here! The Apostle Paul had personally planted this church, spending nearly 3 years there (see Acts 19). Church history tells us that the Apostle John lived there in his later years as the Bishop of Ephesus. Their heritage as an apostolic church was rich and deep. No wonder they had

---

[13]Refer to our chart on the structure of the letters on page 35.

Ephesus

no tolerance for self-proclaimed false apostles. And no wonder Jesus introduced Himself as the One Who walks among "the seven golden lampstands." Their identity

> *"Past heritage does not guarantee present or future blessing. Heritage is our history, not our destiny."*

as a lampstand (especially an apostolic lampstand) was important to them. It was their heritage.

Past heritage does not guarantee present or future blessing. Heritage is our history, not our destiny. Our heritage can become a hindrance if it causes us to love our lampstand more than we love Jesus. The lampstand of our idolatry can be our church, our denomination, our para-church or mission organization, our ethnic heritage or something else. The Lord Jesus knew this about the Ephesians, just as He knows each of our situations. He knows what each of us loves and what's important to us. The real question is this: could

> *"Jesus knows our history, our heritage and our hopes better than we do."*

we and would we walk away from it if Jesus called us to? Jesus knows our history, our heritage and our hopes better than we do. So, He always comes to us in a way that uniquely speaks to each of us and to our situation, whatever it may be.

When Jesus Visits His Church

<u>*'Here's What I Know About What You've Been Doing'*</u>

"I know your deeds and your toil and perseverance, and that you cannot endure evil men, and you put to the test those who call themselves apostles, and they are not, and you found them to be false; and you have perseverance and have endured for My name's sake, and have not grown weary." (2:2-3)

Observation # 2: *Jesus knows what we are "doing" - He knows our "deeds."* The word "deeds" (Greek: <u>ergon</u>) is the common Greek word for "work" or "deeds" and occurs 13 times in the letters to the Seven Churches, making it one of the most important words used to describe the Seven Churches of Asia. Ladd points out that the word *"is a broad term indicating not only good deeds but the entire course of life and conduct."* [14] It appears more than thirty times in the New Testament with reference to the "good deeds" that believers should be doing as part of their walk and witness for Christ. [15]

The truth here is simple yet profound. Jesus knows our deeds, our work. He sees what we are doing. From the least thing we do to the greatest thing we do, none of it escapes

---

[14] Ladd, p. 38.

[15] See for an in-depth study of "good deeds" in the life of the believer see our book **The Least Of These: The Role Of Good Deeds In A Jesus-Shaped Spirituality**, available through our website from Amazon.com.

Ephesus

His notice. The "deeds" of the Ephesians involved toil and perseverance and included a steadfast refusal to endure evil men and the testing of false apostles. All good things. And Jesus knew it.

Observation # 3: *It isn't enough to "work hard" for Jesus, even when we're doing good things.* This passage begins with *"toil which results in weariness"* and ends with the *"weariness that comes from toil."* The word rendered "toil" (Greek: _kopon_) describes a striking or beating, hence, labor to the point of weariness. It's related to the word translated "grown weary" (Greek: _kopiao_) which means to grow weary through toil. Not to put too fine a point on all of this but the Ephesians were hard working people.

And they weren't just working hard. They were also "persevering." As we discovered earlier (page 27), the Greek word translated "persevering" (_hupomone_) communicates a sense of "abiding under," particularly the idea of "abiding under pressure." It is patience under pressure. Or as Barclay describes it, *"courageous galantry which accepts suffering and hardship and loss and turns them into grace and glory."*[16] The idea is *"patience which grows only in trials."* They were not just doing good work, they were doing it under extreme

">... the Ephesians had a problem which threatened it all."

---

[16]William Barclay, ***The Revelation of John***, Volume 1, Revised Edition (Philadelphia: The Westminster Press, 1976), page 62.

When Jesus Visits His Church

pressure and with great courage. They were taking self-proclaimed apostles, putting them to the test like suspect coinage (*peiradzo* - *"to test or assay metal"*), and discovering them to be false, counterfeit. False apostles and false doctrine didn't stand a chance in the Church of Ephesus. But despite their hard work and perseverance, the Ephesians had a problem which threatened it all.

<u>'Here's The Issue I Have With You'</u>

"But I have this against you, that you have left your first love." (2:4)

Observation # 4: *In The Kingdom of God, first things must always come first.* Yeah, I know that sounds redundant. Philosophers even have a fancy word for it: a "tautology" - the needless repetition of a phrase or word without adding any useful information. Where else would "first things" come, you might ask. Second? But sometimes it is the simple-but-critical redundancies of life which we overlook. The Ephesian Christians were working hard with toil and perseverance at things which, on their best day, should rank no higher than third on their priority list. And this wasn't their best day. This was the day when Jesus paid them a visit and revealed to them that they had fallen - dramatically. They had left their first love.

The Greek word translated "left" is a strong word meaning "forsaken" or "abandoned." They had forsaken and abandoned their "first love." But what's that all about? What

Ephesus

is this "first love"? Because we aren't specifically told what this first love is, we have to ask whether or not Scripture has anything to say about the idea of a first love. The good news is, yes, it does. Jesus Himself defined "first love" in Matthew 22:34-40:

*"But when the Pharisees heard that He had put the Sadducees to silence, they gathered themselves together. And one of them, a lawyer, asked Him a question, testing Him, 'Teacher, which is the great commandment in the Law?' And He said to him, 'You shall **love** the Lord your God with all your heart, and with all your soul, and with all your mind. This is the great and **foremost** commandment. The second is like it, You shall **love** your neighbor as yourself. On these two commandments depend the whole Law and the Prophets.'"*

The word translated "foremost" (Greek: *prote*) is the same word rendered "first" in Revelation 2: 4. Could it really be that simple? Was it really possible that the Christians of Ephesus had stopped loving God with all of their heart, mind, soul and strength; had stopped loving their neighbors as themselves; and had replaced intimacy with God and love for others with mere "works?" As Ladd observes, *"Doctrinal purity and loyalty can never be a substitute for love."*[17]

The Ephesians were guilty before the bar of heaven of having failed to keep the two greatest commandments. They

---

[17]Ladd, ***A Commentary On The Revelation Of John***, page 3.

When Jesus Visits His Church

had become overly focused on those works which, as I said earlier, even on a good day, should rank no higher than third on their priority list.

How easily and quickly we forget that life in the Kingdom of God - life in God's Church - is about faith, hope and love expressed and manifested in a life of sacrificial obedience and service to the King, and to others. We live, serve and perform for an "Audience of One."

> *"The Ephesians were guilty before the bar of heaven of having failed to keep the two greatest commandments."*

Writing for **Focus on the Family**, Christian author Ken Gire summed it up well:

"When asked what the secret of living the Christian life was, Augustine replied: 'Love God, and do as you please.' The thought of that is both liberating and confining. Liberating because it means we are free to do whatever we want. Confining because it means our love for God sets the boundaries of that freedom. It guides every thought, every action, every conversation. And it does so every minute of the day, every day of our life. Instead of a Byzantine complexity of laws to regulate every detail of our life, we have only one. The love of God. When that is at the heart of who we are, it changes what we do. And it changes something else. How we will be judged. St. John of the Cross once said that 'at the evening of our day we shall be judged by our

Ephesus

loving.' As we look back over our day, what we have done is not as important as how we have done it. Better to do little with much love than much with little love. For without love, whatever we do will be dismissed with a judicial wave of heaven's hand as just so many trivial pursuits (1 Corinthians 13:1-3)."

<u>'Here's What You Need To Do - Or Else'</u>

"Remember therefore from where you have fallen, and repent and do the deeds you did at first or else I am coming to you, and will remove your lampstand out of its place—unless you repent." (2:5)

Observation # 5: *Repentance is God's prescribed remedy for the sickness of sin and disobedience.* There are actually two steps given here. The first is to "remember" where they have fallen from. The Ephesians needed to remember how, under the ministry of Paul and his passion for Christ, the message of the Kingdom of God had turned Ephesus upside down some forty years earlier. They needed to remember their joy in loving God when the Apostle John had ministered in their midst only a few short years before. They needed to remember the joy of loving God more than anything else. And remembering all those things, they needed to repent for having lost them. Repentance is an important concept in the letters to the Seven Churches. Its eight occurrences in the letters make it one of the dominant themes in Jesus' messages.

When Jesus Visits His Church

Repentance In The Old Testament - The two most common words for "repentance" in the Old Testament are *nacham*, which has to do with a "change of heart or attitude" and *shub* which has to do with a change of behavior or direction (literally: *"to turn, to turn back or to return"*). Repentance in the O.T. meant that you were going in the wrong direction (away from God) and that you needed to make a profound change. You needed to "turn" and to go in the opposite direction (toward God).

Repentance In The New Testament - The New Testament concept of repentance embraces the Old Testament idea of "turning back" but also goes beyond it. The N.T. word for repentance (*metanoia*) describes a profound change of heart and mind which acknowledges one's actions, expresses genuine regret for those actions and their consequences and which produces a wiser view of both the past and the future.[18]

The Importance Of Repentance - Why is "repentance" so important? *First*, it is important because we all get turned in the wrong direction at some point and need to get "turned back" toward God and His will and purposes for our lives. *Second*, it is important because God has established repentance as the 1st step in restoring our relationship with Him. *Third*, it is important because repentance is an

---

[18] For a more in-depth treatment of repentance in Scripture and in the life of the believer, see our book ***The Inextinguishable Blaze: God's Call To Holiness, Repentance, Intimacy and Spiritual Awakening***. Available through our website from Amazon.com.

Ephesus

expression of humility on our part, and God *"opposes the proud but gives grace to the humble"* (1 Peter 5:5).

If you want to get back to where you should be in your relationship with God, it is really pretty simple: **Repent.** Recognize, acknowledge and come to terms with your fallen condition. Turn away from whatever it is that has stolen your gaze and distracted your attention, and get your heart refocused on Jesus.

Observation # 6: *Just as there is a "first love," so there are also "first deeds."* As part of their repentance Jesus tells the Ephesian Church to *"do the first deeds"* (literal Greek rendering). But, like the issue of "first love" the command begs a question: What are the "first deeds"? Does Scripture say? Well, yes, I think so. I believe I found the answer in John 6:28-29:

*"They said therefore to Him, 'What shall we do, that we may work the works of God?' Jesus answered and said to them, This is the **work** of God, that you **believe** in Him whom He has sent."*

The Jews who were questioning Jesus in John 6, had a defective understanding of Jesus and the Kingdom of God. They wanted to make Jesus King so He could set up the Kingdom, vanquish the Romans and give them an endless supply of fish and bread (apparently, this was the only lesson they had taken away from the feeding of the five thousand earlier in Chapter 6). They misunderstood what it meant to

When Jesus Visits His Church

"do the work of God" (a similar problem to that in Ephesus). Jesus confronted this misunderstanding by juxtaposing two competing concepts: "believing" versus "working." The first and greatest "work" (yep, same Greek word for "deed" - *ergon* - as in Revelation 2) any of us will ever do is to simply "believe." The point is simple, clear and profound: in spite of all our "hard work," all of our "deeds," there are no substitutes for **faith** and **love**; the "first deeds" and the "first love."

Observation # 7: *God knows how to "shake us up."* I don't know about you, but this whole "or else" business raises a question in my mind. Why would the Lord Jesus be so hard on Christians and Churches who were working

> *"We live, serve and perform for an Audience of One."*

so hard and persevering under such difficult circumstances? To us, somehow it just doesn't seem "fair." The problem is that life in the Kingdom of God isn't about "fairness" in human terms. Life in the Kingdom of God is about faith, hope and love expressed and manifested in a life of sacrificial obedience and service to the King. We live, serve and perform for an Audience of One.

Unbeknownst to them, like a slow growing cancer of the soul, the Ephesian Christians appear to have lost both their faith and their love, which means they were probably on the verge of losing their hope, too (the blessed hope of the Lord's return and the future hope of eternal life). Can that happen?

Ephesus

You tell me. I am personally appalled by the number of "former-pastors-turned-atheists" who dot the religious landscape - like the one who recently appeared on the local TV news in his police chaplains uniform. A former denominational pastor himself, he was suing the city because the Police Chaplaincy was "too overtly Christian" - apparently unlike himself. Is it remotely possible that the genesis of such declines can be traced to a church like that of Ephesus where "good works for God" had replaced intimacy and love toward God?

Jesus frames His rebuke to the Church of Ephesus in terms which touched that very thing which mattered most to them - the removal of their lampstand. As we noted earlier, for the Ephesians their lampstand was very important to them. They were proud of their heritage as an apostolic lampstand. It represented their identity as a church, which is probably why Jesus threatened it. The word "remove" (Greek: _kino_) can mean either "to shake" or "to remove." When our heritage (our "lampstand") becomes our hindrance, Jesus has no choice but to "shake" it, even remove it, if necessary. Repentance, whether personal or corporate, is how we avoid God having to "shake us up."

<u>'Here's Something Else That I Noticed About You'</u>

Yet this you do have, that you hate the deeds of the Nicolaitans, which I also hate." (2:6)

I'm not going to deal with the Nicolaitans here. They get

When Jesus Visits His Church

extensively treated when Jesus speaks to the Church at Pergamum. For now, let's just agree that anything the Risen Christ "hates" is probably something we want to avoid!

<u>*'Do You Hear What I'm Saying'*</u>

"He who has an ear, let him hear what the Spirit says to the churches." (2:7a)

The word "churches" (plural) tells me that this message (and all the messages to the Seven Churches) wasn't intended only for the Church at Ephesus, or the Church of the 1st Century. Rather, it is a message to the Church of God in every age - and that includes you and me. Good works for God, as important as they may be (and make no mistake, they ARE important), can never replace either loving God with all our heart, soul, mind and strength, or loving our neighbor as ourselves. Jesus' word to the Church in Ephesus is His word to us, too.

<u>*'Just Between You And Me'*</u>

To him who overcomes, I will grant to eat of the tree of life, which is in the Paradise of God." (2:7)

The rewards promised to each of the Seven Churches Of Asia are unique to that Church and to their situation. One of the symbols of the City of Ephesus was the date palm tree. The Risen Christ promises the Ephesian believers a much greater reward than anything living in Ephesus and eating

Ephesus

from its date palms could possibly offer them. He offers them "the tree of life," which is eternal life in the Kingdom of God.

When Jesus Visits Your House Church

As you and your house church prepare for a season of divine visitation, what can you learn from the Church of Ephesus? What do you hear the Holy Spirit saying to you and to the Church in your house through His message to the Church of Ephesus?

1. Loving vs Working. It is possible to lose our spiritual balance while working hard at good things. Are you guilty of "working hard" but "loving little," of having abandoned and forsaken your first love? The high calling of the believer is to love the Lord our God with all of our heart, soul and mind, and our neighbor as ourselves. These are our top two priorities. Everything else, regardless of how important, should place no higher than third on this list of priorities.

2. Heritage vs Calling. Are you guilty of loving your "lampstand" too much? While our history can often explain how we got to where we are, our history does not determine either our present or our future. What is God's calling upon your life and ministry today? And has your heritage become a hindrance to the new thing He wants to do in and through you and your house church?

When Jesus Visits His Church

3. Forgetting, Remembering and Repenting. What have you forgotten, and what do you need to remember about your "first love." Is it time to repent and return?

Remember: *In the Kingdom of God, there is no prize for those who spiritually and morally compromise.*

Smyrna
(Revelation 2:8-11)

"(8) And to the angel of the church in Smyrna write: 'The words of the first and the last, who died and came to life. (9) I know your tribulation and your poverty (but you are rich) and the slander of those who say that they are Jews and are not, but are a synagogue of Satan. (10) Do not fear what you are about to suffer. Behold, the devil is about to throw some of you into prison, that you may be tested, and for ten days you will have tribulation. Be faithful unto death, and I will give you the crown of life. (11) He who has an ear, let him hear what the Spirit says to the churches. The one who conquers will not be hurt by the second death.'"

When Jesus Visits His Church

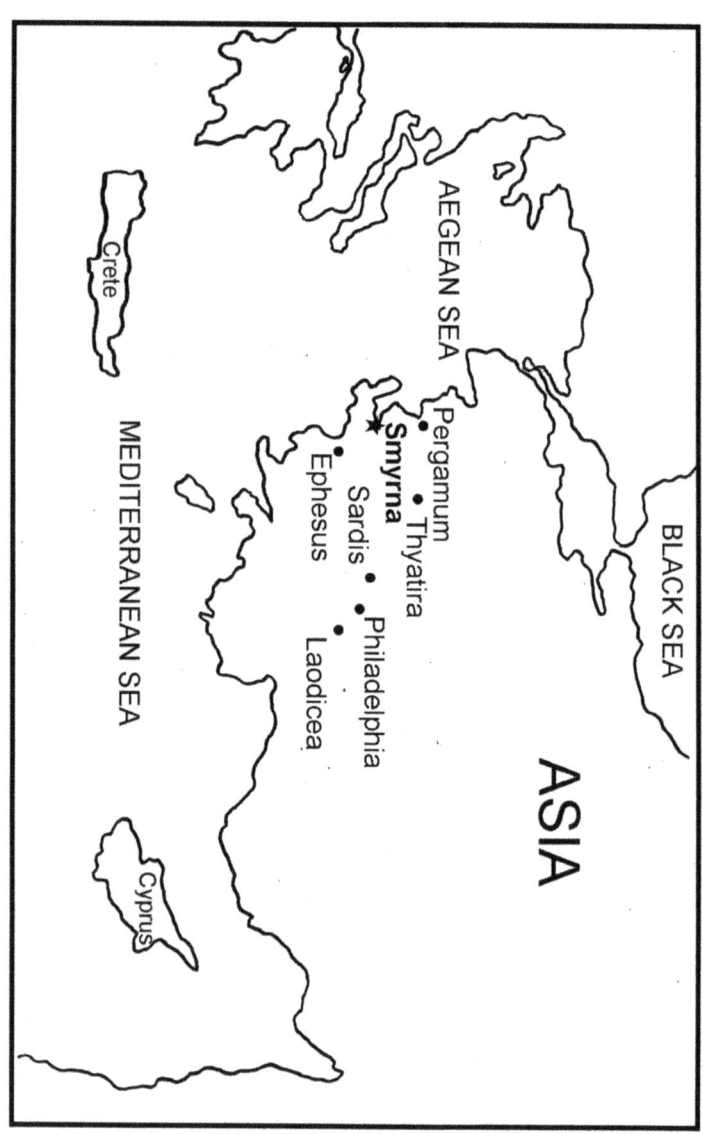

Smyrna

*The Church That Overcame Fear
And Received The Crown of Life
(Revelation 2:8-11)*

Then and Now

The Christians of pre-WW2 Korea would have felt right at home in ancient Smyrna. And therein lies both a story and a lesson of the timeless relevancy of Jesus' Words to the Seven Churches of Asia. The words of the Risen Christ to the 1st century Church of Smyrna were as relevant to the Church of Korea in the first half of the 20th Century as they were to the struggling believers of Smyrna in the last half of the 1st Century.

In 1905 the Japanese Empire defeated the Imperial Russian Navy at the pivotal Battle of Tsushima (fought May 27-28, 1905), effectively ending the Russo-Japanese war of 1904-1905. To the victorious Japanese went the spoils of war, including the Korean Peninsula, which they had occupied during the conflict. Then, in August of 1910, Japan officially annexed Korea, setting in motion a series of events which would test and shake the Church in Korea in ways no one could have foreseen.

Several conflicts marked the relationship between the Korean Church and the Japanese-controlled Korean government, including the "Conspiracy Case" of 1910, the 1919 "Independence Movement," and the education crisis of the 1920 (rooted in education laws passed in 1911). But these

When Jesus Visits His Church

were merely the gathering clouds of an approaching storm. In the years leading up to World War 2 the Japanese Government, pressured by the growing influence of the "military clique," began emphasizing the role of Shinto ('the way of the god') - the ancient Japanese religion of ancestor worship. Specifically, there was an increasing emphasis upon forcing the people of Korea to express their patriotic loyalty by showing reverence to the Japanese Emperor, who was regarded by the Japanese people as a deity. This reverence was accomplished by public participation in Shinto ceremonies and bowing before Shinto shrines. These ceremonies were usually conducted at a "spirit house" (Jinja) where Shinto priests officiated, calling forth spirits and offering prayers to them. The ceremonies were often cloaked as "patriotic" ceremonies ("like pledging allegiance to or saluting the flag" was the official government explanation given to foreign missionaries), but Japanese officials admitted privately, *"The great majority of the Japanese people believe that spirits are being worshiped in the (patriotic Shinto) ceremonies."* [19]

Christians were soon faced with expulsion from school, losing their jobs in schools or government, or the closing of Christian-founded institutions (i.e., hospitals, schools, seminaries, etc.) unless they participated in the ceremonies. Soon, Christians were divided, some seeing and rationalizing

---

[19] See Blair and Hunt, ***The Korean Pentecost and The Suffering Which Followed*** (The Banner of Truth Trust; First Edition, May 1977).

Smyrna

participation in the ceremonies as nothing more significant than laying a wreath at the tomb of "the Unknown Soldier" or saluting the flag. Most missionaries took a strong stand against the ceremonies and mission agencies closed mission schools rather than have students or teachers participate as representatives of the school. Soon there were instances of teachers imprisoned or denied a teaching certificate, and of students expelled from school and imprisoned for refusing to attend the ceremonies.

Originally, the government had represented shrine worship as necessary only for students to make them "loyal and good subjects" (a phrase included in the education law of 1911 which now came back to haunt missionaries, teachers and students). But following Japan's invasion of Manchuria in 1931 (and again after declaring war on China in 1937) the military clique insisted that loyalty must be shown by all subjects through participation in the ceremonies. School children were forced to bow to shrines set up in the school yard and at larger public shrines on special occasions. Public employees were made to bow to shrines in the offices daily and at public shrines on special occasions. Later it was insisted that all public meetings, including such meetings as Presbytery meetings, General Assembly meetings and Women's Missionary Society meetings, be opened with some form of patriotic Shinto bowing.

Penalties for non-participation in the shrine ceremonies (or for open opposition) ranged from moderate to severe. The government kept a "black book" on such people and could

When Jesus Visits His Church

make their lives generally miserable. Things ranging from permits to food rationing cards were denied to "non-co-operators." Children were beaten, expelled from school and imprisoned for refusing to bow at shrines. Informers tracked the movements of missionaries and laymen alike. The Reverend Lloyd Henderson, a Presbyterian missionary was shot and killed while traveling on a moonlit night under Japanese military guard (for his safety!). Reverend Otto De Camp and Dr. D. S. Lowe of the Northern Presbyterian Mission were arrested and imprisoned for removing a small unwanted Japanese shrine from the home of one of the Korean workers living on mission property. They were held in prison and treated like ordinary criminals for several months.

In 1938 the issue of shrine worship was forced on the General Assembly of the Korean Presbyterian Church by the Japanese government. The Government forced the General Assembly to propose and adopt a resolution declaring that shrine worship was permissible and not sinful. Commissioners to the Assembly were personally intimidated in their homes by Government officials and given three options: 1)Attending the Assembly and voting for the resolution, 2) Attending the Assembly but remaining silent on the shrine issue, or 3) Not attending the Assembly. Plain clothes policemen escorted individual Commissioners, armed police guarded every door, and police and government officials oversaw the meeting inside the church. No debate, discussion or dissension was allowed and only affirmative votes were asked for and counted.

Smyrna

Following the "passage" of the resolution the Government renewed its attacks by labeling non-cooperators as individual fanatics who were unwilling to obey the laws and rules of their own church. Korean church leaders were targeted. Many stood firm, willing to pay the heavy toll for their unrelenting and uncompromising faith, but not all. Some fled the country. Others left the ministry and went into secular work. Others went into hiding. Many broke under the unrelenting strain.

Next, the government sought out laymen with convictions, demanding shrine worship in local churches and even in individual homes.

> *"Fear is a natural part of the human condition."*

A pregnant mother and her school-age daughter, a deaconess and her husband with a one-month-old-baby, the 15-year-old son of an evangelist, a mission nurse, an elderly farmer and church leader, all arrested and imprisoned for refusing to worship at a shrine. Arrest, imprisonment, torture, suffering and even death faced these brave martyrs. Scores of Korean Christians died, and multiple scores more suffered for their uncompromising faith. And all learned the timeless meaning of the words which the Risen Christ spoke to the suffering Christians of ancient Smyrna: *"Do not fear what you are about to suffer."*

Fear is a natural part of the human condition. It is no quirk that one of the most frequent divine admonitions to men is "Fear not"! And the fear of death (or of the suffering which

When Jesus Visits His Church

may precede death) is one of the most powerful fears to grip the human heart. The "good news" of the gospel is that Jesus came that He *"might deliver those who through fear of death were subject to slavery all their lives."* (Hebrews 2:15) The Christians of Smyrna were about to discover the reality of this truth as they faced the harsh realities of persecution, suffering and death.

Background of Smyrna

According to the Greek writer and geographer Strabo (64/63 BC – c. AD 24) in his 17-volume *"Geographica,"* Smyrna was a beautiful city with paved streets, a library, a gymnasium, and a shrine to the legendary Homer, who tradition holds may have been born there. Thirty five miles northwest of Ephesus, Smyrna was the chief seaport of Asia. In addition to its importance as a trading center, Smyrna was a long-time friend of Rome. Smyrna had worshiped the spirit of Rome as early as 195 B.C. In the year AD 26 some eleven cities competed for the honor of building a temple to *"the spirit of Rome and the genius of the Emperor."* In its application Smyrna cited its close historic ties to Rome. According to the Roman historian Tacitus,

"They had aided Rome with a naval force, they said, not only in their wars abroad, but also in those they had fought in Italy. It was they, they said, who had first reared a temple in honor of Rome, when the power of the Roman people, though great, had not yet reached their highest glory, for the city of Carthage still stood, and powerful kings governed

Smyrna

Asia." (Tacitus, *Annals*, 4.56)

Smyrna was chosen as the site of the second Asian temple to Rome and the Emperor, thereby establishing itself as an active seat for the rising cult of emperor worship.

> *"When you are facing issues of life and death, it's a good thing to know the One Who has conquered both and can empower you to do the same."*

The new temple to Rome and the Emperor Tiberius increased the pride she felt in this role, and the resentment she felt toward anyone who - like the early Christian church - might question or challenge that role.

Roughly 60 years after the book of Revelation, in the year AD 156, the elderly Bishop Polycarp, a disciple of the Apostle John, was martyred in Smyrna for refusing to offer the pinch of incense and declaring, "Caesar is Lord." Polycarp was the 12th martyr in a persecution of Christians carried out by the Roman authorities and encouraged by the local Jewish community, which the Risen Christ describes as *"a synagogue of Satan."*

<u>'Here's Who I Am In Relation To You'</u>

"And to the angel of the church in Smyrna write: 'The words of the first and the last, who died and came to life." (2:8)

The Risen Christ introduces Himself in that unique way which

When Jesus Visits His Church

would be most meaningful to the Christians of Smyrna - as the One who has conquered death with life. Why was this important? Because the Risen Christ knew that the Christians of Smyrna were facing life and death issues at the hands of the Roman Government, and persecution at the hands of an antagonistic and hostile Jewish community. When you are facing issues of life and death, it's a good thing to know the One Who has conquered both and can empower you to do the same.

'Here's What I know About What You've Been Doing'

"I know your tribulation and your poverty (but you are rich) and the slander of those who say that they are Jews and are not, but are a synagogue of Satan. Do not fear what you are about to suffer. Behold, the devil is about to throw some of you into prison, that you may be tested, and for ten days you will have tribulation. Be faithful unto death, and I will give you the crown of life." (2:9-10)

This was a Church which had already experienced difficult times:

1. They had experienced "tribulation" - *"the pressure of crushing distress"* - and Jesus was well aware of it.

2. They had experienced "poverty" (*ptocheia* - *"extreme poverty, beggary, destitution, indigence"*). This same Greek word is found in 2 Corinthians 8. Like the Macedonians who gave sacrificially to Paul's ministry out of great poverty, the

Smyrna

Christians of Smyrna were destitute by the world's standards, but they were rich in a way that the world and its money could never measure.

3. They had been vilified and slandered (_blasphemeo_ - _"to vilify, defame rail against, revile; to speak impiously"_) at the hands of Jewish persecutors whom the Risen Christ labels "a synagogue of Satan."

The response of the Risen Christ to what they had experienced is simple but profound: _"I Know . . ."_ Jesus is well aware of everything you have been through. He knows.

> ". . . the Christians of Smyrna were destitute by the world's standards, but they were rich in a way that the world and its money could never measure."

This was a Church for whom difficult times were about to increase:

The Christians of Smyrna were _"about to suffer"_ (_pascha_ - _"passion, suffering"_). They were about to experience the practical effects of spiritual warfare. They were about to be persecuted and cast into prison. Note that, according to the Risen Christ, it was not the Romans but the Devil who was about to do this. In other words, this represented spiritual warfare with practical consequences. Their personal and spiritual metal was about to be tested (_peiradzo_ - _"to_

When Jesus Visits His Church

examine, test or assay metal") under the extreme pressure of tribulation in the form of persecution, imprisonment and suffering. Some of them

> *"All men die. The only issue for the believer is the circumstances under which they die."*

were about to die for their faith. And that kind of pressure is enough to strike fear into the heart of any man or woman.

All men die. The only issue for the believer is the circumstances under which they die. The good news was that their tribulation was only going to be for a season (i.e., "ten days"). Nothing lasts forever . . . except eternity with Christ.

"Fear Not" - In the face of what they are "about to suffer," the Risen Christ exhorts them: *"Do not be afraid."* Scripture has much to say about fear, nearly all of which can be summarized into two basic types of fear: **servile** and **sanctified**. [20]

Servile fear is any fear of people, places, things or circumstances apart from God. The human heart is prone to many fears in this fallen world: fear of the unknown, fear of men (and what they can do to us), fear of want and suffering, disaster, sickness and, perhaps the greatest fear of all, the

---

[20]The simple phrase *"Do not be afraid"* occurs no less than 33 times in Scripture (the phrase *"fear not"* also occurs some 33 times), mostly in passages where God is encouraging people to not be afraid.

Smyrna

fear of death. The Christians in Smyrna were facing all of these fears at once.

"Is the fear in your life a servile fear of people and circumstances, or a sanctified fear of God?"

The list of things which strike fear into the human heart is as endless and varied as the number of people in the world. But they all have one thing in common. They all have the power to distract us, enslave us, paralyze us and prevent us from obeying God and enjoying the blessing of obedience to His will. All such fears are the collective enemy of the Kingdom of God, and of our discipleship.

Sanctified fear is the type of fear which Scripture encourages, namely, *"the fear of the Lord."* No less than 25 Scriptures teach the blessings of *"the fear of the Lord."* And the man or woman who truly fears God will not fear any man, or any man-imposed persecution.

"Be Faithful" - This letter breaks the "pattern" of the seven letters in that it contains no rebuke or admonishment (of the 7 Churches, 2 receive no rebuke: Smyrna and Philadelphia). The Christians of Smyrna were about to suffer terribly, and many would die. The Risen Christ understood this. Men facing pain, suffering and death need no rebuke. They need encouragement and a prize worth dying for, which is exactly what Jesus gave them: *"Fear not . . . . Be faithful . . . . And I will give you the crown of life."* The "crown" or <u>stephanos</u> here was NOT a crown symbolizing "royalty," but the trophy

When Jesus Visits His Church

awarded to the victor at the games (especially since Smyrna was also famous for its games). But the "Crown of Life" offered by the Risen Christ to those who suffer for His sake is greater than any "crown of men" that this world may have to offer. As Ladd notes, *"The crown itself is eternal life."* [21]

'Do You Hear What I'm Saying'

"He who has an ear, let him hear what the Spirit says to the churches." (2:11a)

What is the Holy Spirit saying? Like the message to the Church at Ephesus, the message to the Church at Smyrna is timeless, *"Don't be afraid to suffer or even die for Christ."* Throughout the history of the Church, from the persecution of Christians by the Roman Empire to the persecution of believers today in Muslim countries, the message is clear and consistent: *"Fear not, and be faithful . . . even unto death."*

'Just Between You And Me'

"He who overcomes shall not be hurt by the second death." (2:11b)

This is one of those times when the reward of the Risen Christ to the Church can be understood and appreciated by all of us. Many believers in the Church of Smyrna were about

---

[21]Ladd, ***A Commentary On The Revelation Of John***, page 45.

Smyrna

to die, and everyone in the Church there was facing the fear of persecution and death. Every person faces two deaths: One physical, and one spiritual. Everyone **must** die physically; we have no choice in the matter. The only question surrounding our physical death is the matter of timing and circumstances ("when" and "how"). But whether or not we experience the "second death" (which is "the lake of fire" or "hell") is a matter of our choice (Revelation 2:11; 20:6, 14; 21:8).

When Jesus Visits Your House Church

As you and your house church prepare for a season of divine visitation, what can you learn from the Church of Smyrna? What do you hear the Holy Spirit saying to you and to the Church in your house through His message to the Church of Smyrna?

1. "I Know..." - What do you think the Risen Christ already knows about what you have already experienced on His behalf? How do you think He responds to what He knows about your life?

2. Fear Not! - What are you afraid of? How does the stronghold of fear manifest in your life? Is the fear in your life a servile fear of men and circumstances? Or is it a sanctified fear of God? What is He saying to you regarding the issue of fear in your life? The only "fear" that Scripture speaks positively about is the sanctified "fear of God." A genuine sense of the fear of God was a characteristic of the New

When Jesus Visits His Church

Testament church (see Acts 2:43; 5:11). Throughout the history of the Church, seasons of spiritual outpouring and divine visitation have been times when the fear of God has replaced the fear of men in the lives of believers. What about you? Has the fear of God replaced the fear of men in your life?

3. Be Faithful! - Active faithfulness during difficult times is one of the things which secures for each of us "the crown." And so the Risen Christ says to each of us and to His Church: *"If you want the crown, you have to compete in the game."* How is the Risen Christ calling you and your house church to greater faithfulness today?

Remember: *In the Kingdom of God, there is no prize for those who spiritually and morally compromise.*

Pergamum
(Revelation 2:12-17)

(12) "And to the angel of the church in Pergamum write: 'The words of him who has the sharp two-edged sword. (13) I know where you dwell, where Satan's throne is. Yet you hold fast my name, and you did not deny my faith even in the days of Antipas my faithful witness, who was killed among you, where Satan dwells. (14) But I have a few things against you: you have some there who hold the teaching of Balaam, who taught Balak to put a stumbling block before the sons of Israel, so that they might eat food sacrificed to idols and practice sexual immorality. (15) So also you have some who hold the teaching of the Nicolaitans. (16) Therefore repent. If not, I will come to you soon and war against them with the sword of my mouth. (17) He who has an ear, let him hear what the Spirit says to the churches. To the one who conquers I will give some of the hidden manna, and I will give him a white stone, with a new name written on the stone that no one knows except the one who receives it.'"

When Jesus Visits His Church

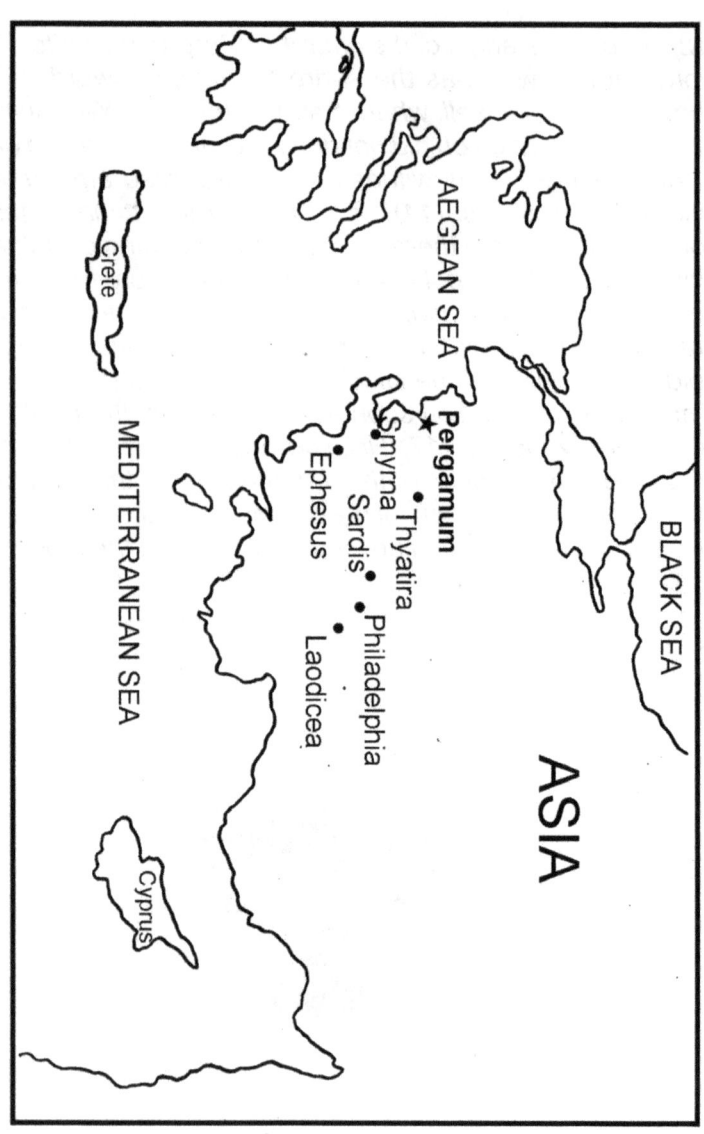

Pergamum
A Compromised Church
(Revelation 2:12-17)

Our Situation Has Not Improved!

Maybe you remember the scene from the movie, *"Indiana Jones And The Last Crusade."* Indiana and his father are stuck in a revolving fireplace which revolves between a room on fire and a room filled with Nazis who want to kill them. After a rotation through this dilemma, Indiana's father remarks, *"Our situation has not improved!"* Yep, some days the spiritual battle is like that. Now you know how the church at Pergamum must have felt. And therein lies a story of compromise, hard choices and repentance.

Background of Pergamum

Built on a series of terraces leading up to its acropolis, the city of Pergamum was the capital seat of the ancient Kingdom of Pergamum, When the last King of Pergamum died in 133 B.C. he bequeathed the Kingdom to Rome. It became the chief town and the capital city in the new Roman Province of Asia. Pergamum became a center of pagan religion and Imperial Caesar-worship.

The first temple of the Roman Imperial cult, a temple to Rome and the emperor Augustus, was built there in 29 B.C. It attained the coveted title of *knackwurst* or "Temple-sweeper" before either Smyrna or Ephesus achieved that honor. Pergamum took devotion to the cult of Emperor

When Jesus Visits His Church

Worship seriously and was the principal center of the Imperial cult in that part of the world.

"Observance of this worship (of the Emperor) became a test of loyalty to Rome, for the imperial cult was the keystone of the imperial policy, and refusal to take part in the official cult was considered high treason." [22]

Pergamum was also home to numerous other deities, including a temple to Asklepios, the god of healing, whose symbol was a serpent. Asklepios is described as *"sitting on a throne with a staff in his hand, and his other hand upon the head of a serpent."* And sitting on a bluff-terrace of the 1,000 foot high acropolis overlooking the city sat the colossal altar of Zeus.

<u>'Here's Who I Am In Relation To You'</u>

"And to the angel of the church in Pergamum write: The One who has the sharp two-edged sword says this . . ." (2:12a)

As we learned during our look at the Church of Ephesus, Jesus introduces Himself to each church in a manner unique to each particular church. To the Church at Pergamum the Risen Christ introduces himself as *"the One Who has the sharp two-edged sword."* Why was this special? Because Jesus wasn't the only person in Pergamum who wielded a two-edged sword. So did Caesar. When it comes to religious

---

[22]Ladd, ***A Commentary On The Revelation Of John***, page 45.

Pergamum

persecution, Smyrna and Pergamum had situations which were quite similar. But the message of Jesus to each was quite

> *"We are all different in our responses to the challenges set before us, and Jesus deals with us as individuals."*

different. Why? Because two Christians can face the same problem or circumstance, yet struggle with it very differently. The believers of Smyrna struggled with fear and death in their confrontation with the imperial cult, while the believers of Pergamum struggled with compromise in the face of the same threat. We are all different in our responses to the challenges set before us, and Jesus deals with us as individuals.

'Here's What I Know About What You've Been Doing'

"I know where you dwell, where Satan's throne is. Yet you hold fast my name, and you did not deny my faith even in the days of Antipas my faithful witness, who was killed among you, where Satan dwells."(2:12-13)

As we have already observed, Pergamum was the administrative center of the Roman province of Asia. It had the twin distinction of being a center for the Imperial cult of Caesar worship, as well as the home of the great temple and altar of Zeus, situated on a hillside from which it overlooked and dominated the city. To those Christians who lived in the city below, it really must have looked like "Satan's Throne." Satan ruled this town, with help from the Romans.

When Jesus Visits His Church

The profession of Christianity had been forbidden by law throughout the Empire since the days of Nero, some thirty years earlier. Christians who refused to offer incense at a bust of Caesar while declaring "Caesar is Lord" were subject to the sword . . . or worse. Apparently, that's what happened to Antipas (or "Antipater") whom church tradition says died, not by the sword, but by being placed inside a bronze bull and burned to death during the reign of the Emperor Domitian (circa A.D. 81). Ouch! Yep, life was a little on the challenging side for believers who lived *"where Satan dwells."* They were confronted daily with rampant, even satanic, paganism (often involving temple prostitution) on the one hand, and state mandated and enforced idolatry on the other. Like Indiana Jones in a revolving fireplace, their situation was not much improved! In fact, it was about to get worse.

> *"Integrity in the Christian life is often defined and determined by how we respond to difficult, even impossible, situations."*

Integrity in the Christian life is often defined and determined by how we respond to difficult, even impossible, situations. And the integrity of the believers in Pergamum was being severely tested.

<u>'Here's The Issue I Have With You'</u>

"But I have a few things against you: you have some there who hold the teaching of Balaam, who taught Balak to put a

Pergamum

stumbling block before the sons of Israel, so that they might eat food sacrificed to idols and practice sexual immorality. So also you have some who hold the teaching of the Nicolaitans." (2:14-15).

The Nicolaitans

It seems that the Nicolaitans, which the Ephesian Church had successfully opposed, had gained a foothold in the Church of Pergamum. As this passage suggests, there is a connection between the Nicolaitans of the New Testament and the episode with Balaam in the Old Testament, so that is where we need to go next.

Balaam, Balak and The Israelites. O.K., this will take some "unpacking." The whole sordid affair with Balak (King of the Moab) and Balaam took place during the 40-year "wilderness wandering" episode of Israel's Old Testament history. You can read the account in the book of Numbers, chapters 22-25 (to pique your interest, it involved frightened Kings, lots of money, a talking donkey and a sword-wielding angel - details to follow). It all culminates in Numbers 25 where we learn that the sons of Israel *"began to play the harlot"* (i.e., engage in illicit sex) with the women of Moab and Median, and to eat things sacrificed to their gods. Balaam himself was eventually killed when Israel destroyed Median (see Numbers 31:8 and Joshua 13:22).

Balaam's Three Bad Lessons. In His message to the Christians at Pergamum, the Risen Christ reduced the above

When Jesus Visits His Church

incident to its basics. Balaam taught (imperfect tense in the Greek, "continually taught") Balak and his people to do three things in order to destroy the people of God:

1. Throw stumbling blocks before them, specifically,

2. Get them to eat food offered or sacrificed to an idol. In other words, get them to stumble over the issue of idolatry - not unlike the problem Paul had to deal with in the Church of Corinth (see 1 Corinthians 8), and,

3. Encourage them to engage in illicit sex. Sexual purity in all its forms is one of the distinctive marks of genuine biblical faith, and Scripture sees a direct relationship between spiritual adultery (idolatry) and sexual adultery.

Balaam, Pergamum and The Nicolaitans. So, what's all this got to do with the Church in Pergamum? Enter the Nicolaitans. The word "nicolaitans" is a compound word, formed from two words: _nikao_, which means "to conquer" or "to rule over" and _laos_, which means "people." Hence, *"to conquer and rule over the people."* Interestingly, the Old Testament name Balaam is derived from two Hebrew words: _bela_ which meant "to conquer" and _ha'am_, meaning "the people." Balaam and the Nicolaitans share the same spirit of conquering people through false teaching and compromise.

Simply put, Balaam was a "false teacher" (in addition to being a false prophet!) who taught Balak how to "conquer" God's people by leading them into temptation and compromise.

Pergamum

False teaching and compromise represent the "linchpin" which connects Balaam and the Nicolaitans. Both situations involved false teachers who "conquered" and "ruled over" God's people with false teaching which led them into compromise and bondage. According to the church father Irenaeus, the Nicolaitans were followers of Nicholas of Antioch who had abandoned right doctrine (yes, doctrine is important - even in house church) and had both taught and lived "unrestrained indulgence." Hippolytus agreed and noted that the Nicolaitans practiced "indifference" regarding what a man ate or how he lived.

Scandalous Indifference and Compromise. Unlike Ephesus, it appears that in Pergamum this false teaching of indifference toward sin had taken root and had led to compromise with the Imperial Cult of Caesar worship. The Nicolaitans taught that, when confronted, Christians could avoid Caesar's sword through indifference toward and compromise with the sin of idolatry. Remember the Bishop in the movie *"Kingdom of Heaven"* who, when standing on the brink of annihilation at the hands of the Muslims, counsels the Christian General, *"Convert now, repent later"*? The Risen Christ, speaking through the Apostle John, understood that, like Balaam, the teaching of the Nicolaitans would

> *"It seems that God understands something here that we do not, namely, spiritual unfaithfulness eventually leads to moral unfaithfulness."*

When Jesus Visits His Church

become a stumbling block, a "scandal" (Greek: _skandalon_). It would produce "scandalous indifference" toward sin and would lead the people of God into compromise, idolatry and more. In both the Old and New Testaments, compromise and idolatry are frequently related to moral impurity. It seems that God understands something here that we do not, namely, spiritual unfaithfulness eventually leads to moral unfaithfulness.

Jesus' admonition to the Christians at Pergamum is blunt, unequivocal and necessary. Like Indiana Jones in a revolving fireplace, you must choose: face Caesar's sword as the

> "Indifference and compromise are sin, because whatever is not of faith is sin (Romans 14:23)."

price for your faithfulness to Christ, or face Christ's sword as the price for your unfaithfulness and compromise with Caesar and paganism. And, no, He never said it would be easy; only that it would be better . . . and that He would be with us.

Here's What You Need To Do - Or Else

"Repent therefore; or else I am coming to you quickly, and I will make war against them with the sword of My mouth." (2:16)

Indifference and compromise are sin, because whatever is not of faith is sin (Romans 14:23). Indifference and compromise are also affronts to God's holiness (which we

Pergamum

are to share and emulate) because they suggest that God is indifferent to sin and is willing to compromise with sin (which He is NOT!). The solution to this dilemma, like the solution to all such dilemmas of sin, indifference and compromise, is simple: **Repent**. Genuine personal (and corporate) repentance is the God-appointed means of seeking Christ's forgiveness and of throwing ourselves upon the mercy of our God. As David discovered during the nasty episode of conducting a forbidden census (1 Chronicles 21), it is always better to cast oneself upon the fathomless ocean of God's mercy, than to place oneself into the hands of men (1 Chronicles 21:13).

<u>Do You Hear What I'm Saying?</u>

"He who has an ear, let him hear what the Spirit says to the churches." (2:17a)

What is the Spirit saying to the Church today through this word to the Church at Pergamum? Is the Church today struggling with false teachers who advocate compromise and "scandalous indifference" toward the sins of our culture?

<u>'Just Between You And Me'</u>

"To him who overcomes, to him I will give some of the hidden manna, and I will give him a white stone, and a new name written on the stone which no one knows but he who receives it." (2:17b)

When Jesus Visits His Church

To the faithful believers in Pergamum the Risen Christ offers "hidden manna." We know about the manna which God gave the Israelites in the wilderness for 40 years, and we know that Jesus described Himself as the true manna from God (John Chapter 6). To the persecuted believers in Pergamum the Risen Christ promises that just as God sustained Israel with manna in the wilderness, Jesus Himself - the true manna from heaven - will sustain them with "hidden manna" during times of persecution and beyond.[23]

In the ancient world Roman juries sometimes gave their verdict by voting with colored stones: a white stone stood for innocent and a black one for guilty. Black stones were used to identify condemned prisoners and white stones were given to those set free. Jesus' promise of a "white stone" could be seen as declaring believers "innocent" on the Day of Judgment. Another possibility is the ancient custom of giving pebbles of various colors as admission tickets and place holders at public celebrations. Victors in the games were given white stones for their admission to the festivities. Perhaps the Risen Christ is promising faithful believers in Pergamum admission to the festivities celebrating his return (the Marriage Supper of the Lamb). What we know without any doubt is that Jesus Himself will reward faithfulness that

---

[23]Ladd, ***A Commentary On The Revelation Of John***, page 49: *"Hebrew tradition held that a pot of manna was preserved in the ark . . . . and when the temple was destroyed, Jeremiah . . . or an angel . . . rescued the ark with the manna, and they were miraculously preserved until the messianic times, when the mana would become once again food for God's people."*

Pergamum

does not compromise!

When Jesus Visits Your House Church

As you and your house church prepare for a season of divine visitation in spiritual awakening, what do you hear the Holy Spirit saying to you through His message to the Church of Pergamum?

Indifference And Compromise - The believers in Pergamum had fallen into spiritual compromise through indifference toward sin. Have you become indifferent to sin and its consequences? Are you counseling others to do the same? Indifference is often the convenient choice in a hostile world. But indifference toward sin to avoid hard choices means compromising our faith and our witness in order to please the world. The solution is simple: Acknowledge your compromise, confess your sin, **and repent**.

Nicolaitans vs Leadership - The issue of "the Nicolaitans" is **NOT** about churches not having leaders over them. It is about BAD leaders and false teachers who offer bad counsel and cause God's people to be indifferent toward sin and the hard moral choices which we as believers must make as part of our witness for Christ in a hostile and fallen world. Spend some time reflecting on the difference between a "Nicolaitan" and a godly, biblical "leader."

Remember: *In the Kingdom of God, there is no prize for those who spiritually and morally compromise.*

When Jesus Visits His Church

Thyatira

(Revelation 2:18-29)

"(18)And to the angel of the church in Thyatira write: The words of the Son of God, who has eyes like a flame of fire, and whose feet are like burnished bronze. (19) "I know your works, your love and faith and service and patient endurance, and that your latter works exceed the first. (20) But I have this against you, that you tolerate that woman Jezebel, who calls herself a prophetess and is teaching and seducing my servants to practice sexual immorality and to eat food sacrificed to idols. (21) I gave her time to repent, but she refuses to repent of her sexual immorality. (22) Behold, I will throw her onto a sickbed, and those who commit adultery with her I will throw into great tribulation, unless they repent of her works, (23) and I will strike her children dead. And all the churches will know that I am he who searches mind and heart, and I will give to each of you according to your works. (24) But to the rest of you in Thyatira, who do not hold this teaching, who have not learned what some call the deep things of Satan, to you I say, I do not lay on you any other burden. (25) Only hold fast what you have until I come. (26) The one who conquers and who keeps my works until the end, to him I will give authority over the nations, (27) and he will rule them with a rod of iron, as when earthen pots are broken in pieces, even as I myself have received authority from my Father. (28) And I will give him the morning star. (29) He who has an ear, let him hear what the Spirit says to the churches.'"

When Jesus Visits His Church

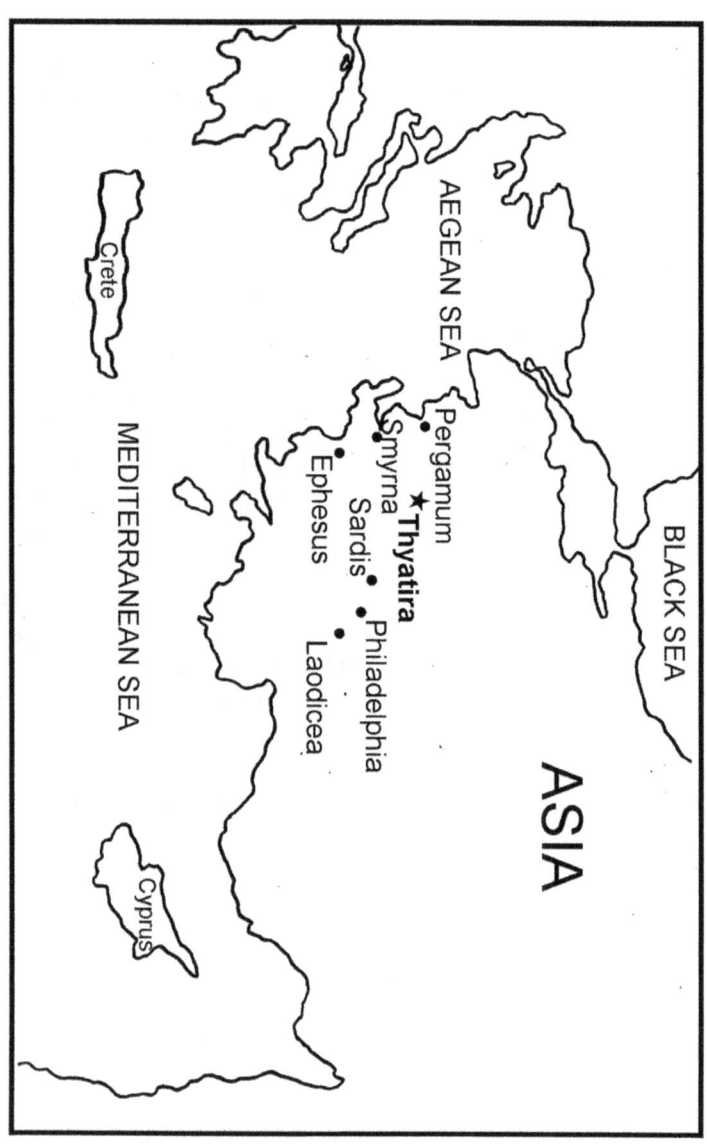

Thyatira

*The Church That Tolerated
False Authority, Witchcraft
and Immorality
(Revelation 2:18-29)*

It was April of 1521 in the German town of Worms (pronounced "vorms"). The Imperial Diet under Holy Roman Emperor Charles V had gathered, along with much of the hierarchy of the Medieval Church, in order to hear and pass judgment upon the views of an obscure Augustinian Monk and Professor of Bible from the University of Wittenburg. The problem had begun four years earlier when this monk had challenged to debate the Church's theology concerning indulgences - a challenge nailed to the door of the University Cathedral where all such public notices were posted.

The Archbishop of Mainz complained to Rome. Next came a confrontation with Cardinal Cajetan in Augsburg (1518) where this defiant monk refused to recant his views. The following year (1519) he disputed the Papal Legate, Cardinal Eck, in Leipzig. Fearing a trap, he fled town when summoned to Rome to explain himself before his supreme spiritual authority, the Pope. The following year he was excommunicated by his "spiritual authority" (the Pope and Church), to which the recalcitrant monk responded by publicly burning the Papal "Bull."

Finally, he had been invited, no summoned, by the Church and the Holy Roman Emperor (under a promise of safe conduct), to appear before the Imperial Diet at Worms to

When Jesus Visits His Church

present and defend his views. And so he did. There Dr. Martin Luther stood. Abandoned and condemned by all of his "spiritual authorities," the "rebellious" and recalcitrant monk declared:

"Your Imperial Majesty and Your Lordships demand a simple answer. Here it is, plain and unvarnished. Unless I am convicted of error by the testimony of Scripture or (since I put no trust in the unsupported authority of the pope or of councils, since it is plain that they have often erred and often contradicted themselves) by manifest reasoning, I stand convicted by the Scriptures to which I have appealed, and my conscience is taken captive by God's Word, I cannot and will not recant anything. For to act against our conscience is neither safe for us, nor open to us. On this I take my stand, I can do no other. God help me. Amen."

God did help him, and the Protestant Reformation was born in earnest. Martin Luther understood something about spiritual authority which many Christians today appear to have forgotten: *God alone* is our "covering." *Scripture alone* is our authority. *Grace alone* is sufficient for all our needs. *Faith alone* opens the door to salvation. And each and every believer is a Priest before God, in need of NO ONE to cover, intercede or mediate between them and God except our Great High Priest, Jesus Christ. False leaders, false teachers, false shepherds and false prophets prey upon people who do not understand this truth, seeking to exercise over people an authority they do not possess. This was the situation in Thyatira where a false-prophetess-turned-teacher

Thyatira

named "Jezebel" was causing believers to stumble.

Background of Thyatira

As the ESV Study Bible observes, *"Thyatira was a politically and economically marginalized city."* Regarding Thyatira, William Barclay noted, *"It is an odd fact that the longest of the letters to the Seven Churches was written to the church in the smallest and least important of the seven towns."*[24] Pliny, The Elder, the Roman jurist and later Governor of Bythinia, dismissed the city of Thyatira with contempt in the phrase, *"Thyatira and other unimportant communities."*

Thyatira was an ancient city founded by the Lydians. In Roman times it was a busy center of commerce, and many of the people there were Jewish settlers. Situated at the intersection of two valleys, it was an important trade route and a Roman garrison was stationed there to protect it. As an important trade junction, a bustling market developed which included dyed cloth and garments, and the manufacture of bronze armor. A coin from Thyatira shows Hephaestus, the "divine smith," hammering a helmet on an anvil.

But Thyatira was best known for the trade of its famous purple cloth. Thyatirian purple cloth became known all over the world and was used in royal dress. In Philippi the Apostle Paul met a merchant woman who bought and sold Thyatiran

---

[24]William Barclay, **Letters To The Seven Churches** (New York: Abington Press, 1957), page 55.

When Jesus Visits His Church

dyed cloth and garments, *"And a certain woman named Lydia, from the city of Thyatira, a seller of purple fabrics, a worshiper of God, was listening; and the Lord opened her heart to respond to the things spoken by Paul"* (Acts 16:14).

The bustling business of Tyatira was organized around trade guilds. More trade guilds have been identified in Thyatira than in any other Asian city. Inscriptions mention workers in wool, linen, leather, bronze, dyers, tanners, potters and bankers. These trade guilds met regularly to celebrate their patron gods. They were close knit communities which met for worship, to discuss trade matters and hold a business dinner, a common meal which was, in part, a religious ceremony. It might meet in the temple of a local god and begin with an offering to the gods. The meal itself might consist largely of meat that had been sacrificed or offered to the god.

This presented a problem for the Christians of Thyatira. In order to make a living at their craft they had to belong to a guild. But a Christian craftsman could hardly attend the formal guild meetings and banquets without witnessing and participating in illicit sex, licentious behavior and idolatry. And it would be difficult - if not impossible - to abstain from the guild festivities without losing one's business and social standing.

<u>'Here's Who I Am In Relation To You'</u>

"And to the angel of the church in Thyatira write:The Son of God, who has eyes like a flame of fire, and His feet are like

Thyatira

burnished bronze, says this . . ." (2:18)

If you thought for a moment that this passage sounded vaguely familiar, you were right. Here the risen Christ describes himself to the Church of Thyatira in the same terms as the awe-inspiring figure who appeared to Daniel: *"I lifted my eyes and looked, and behold, there was a certain man dressed in linen, whose waist was girded with a belt of pure gold of Uphaz. His body also was like beryl, his face had the appearance of lightning, his eyes were like flaming torches, his arms and feet like the gleam of polished bronze, and the sound of his words like the sound of a tumult."* (Daniel 10:5-6)

This image of Christ was intended to evoke "fear and awe" among the believers of Thyatira, just as it did for Daniel. Why?

> *"God's true authority over His Church is rooted not in His omnipotent power, but in His awesome Holiness."*

Because Jesus needed to get their undivided attention and to re-establish His sole authority to speak into their lives. They were having problems with the issue of false authority, and problems with false authority always have their roots in a misunderstanding of God's true authority over us in Christ.

God's true authority over His Church is rooted not in His omnipotent power, but in His awesome Holiness (see Isaiah 6:1ff). *"Be holy, for I am holy,"* is God's standing instruction to His people in every age. But there are times in the life of

When Jesus Visits His Church

His people when God must move in great holiness and fear in order to re-establish His true authority in our lives and in the life of His Church. In the Old Testament we see this in Isaiah 6 and Isaiah's encounter with God's holiness in the Temple. In the New Testament we see this in the events surrounding Ananias and Sapphira in Acts 5:1-10. As a result of those events, God demonstrated His authority to punish sin in His Church. In the process He taught the Church something about His awesome holiness and the genuine, sanctified "fear of God" such holiness evokes, *"And great fear came upon the whole church, and upon all who heard of these things"* (Acts 5:11).

<u>*'Here's What I Know About What You've Been Doing'*</u>

'I know your deeds, and your love and faith and service and perseverance, and that your deeds of late are greater than at first.' (2:19)

The deeds of the Christians in Thyatira included both love and faith, both of which were missing in the Church at Ephesus. In other words, the Christians of Thyatira possessed what the Christians of Ephesus lacked! In addition, the Christians of Thyatira were living as "servants" (<u>*diakonia*</u> - service, ministry, deaconate) to those around them. As Christians, our calling is to be "servants." As "servants," there is nothing wrong with good deeds done out of love and faith. Furthermore, the deeds of Thyatira weren't only good, they were increasing. It seems that the Church of Thyatira had everything that Ephesus lacked. So, what was

Thyatira

the problem?

<u>'Here's The Issue I Have With You'</u>

"But I have this against you, that you tolerate the woman Jezebel, who calls herself a prophetess, and she teaches and leads My bond-servants astray, so that they commit acts of immorality and eat things sacrificed to idols. 'And I gave her time to repent; and she does not want to repent of her immorality.(2:20-21)

The strengths and weaknesses of the Church in Thyatira were the exact opposites of those in Ephesus. The Church in Thyatira was strong in love as evidenced by their works. But unlike the believers in Ephesus, the believers in Thyatira lacked discernment and they tolerated heresy. *"The problem in Thyatira was an unhealthy tolerance. They recognized the presence of the false prophetess; they recognized also the evil character of her teaching, but they tolerantly refused to deal with her."* [25]

Background Regarding "Jezebel"

The problem in Thyatira revolved around a woman who was a self-proclaimed "prophetess," referred to here as "Jezebel" (probably NOT her name, but her "description"). This requires some "unpacking."

---

[25] Ladd, ***A Commentary On The Revelation Of John***, page 51.

When Jesus Visits His Church

According to 1 Kings 16:31 Jezebel was the daughter of Ethbaal, King of Zidon (Sidon). The region of Sidon was a "hot-bed" of pagan Baal worship. So, Ahab, King of the northern Kingdom of Israel, who was already in rebellion against Jehovah and walking *"in the sins of Jeroboam the son of Nebat,"* married a pagan, religious Baal worshiper, who *"went and served Baal, and worshiped him."* To make a long story short, Jezebel came to be known for seven (7) things:

1. She was a religious Baal worshiper (1 Kings 16:31),
2. She killed ("cut off") the Prophets of Jehovah (1 Kings 18:4),
3. She fed and provided for 400 prophets of Baal (1 Kings 18:19),
4. She waged personal warfare against Elijah (1 Kings 19:1-2),
5. She plotted with her husband, Ahab, to kill Naboth and steal his vineyard (1 Kings 21:1-15),
6. She stirred up Ahab *"to work wickedness in the sight of the Lord"* (1 Kings 21:25),
7. She practiced *"witchcrafts"* (2 Kings 9:22).

Like her Old Testament name-sake, the problem with Jezebel in the Church of Thyatira can basically be summed up as rebellion and false authority. Deuteronomy 18:10 says, *"There shall not be found among you anyone who makes his son or his daughter pass through the fire, one who uses divination, one who practices, witchcraft, or one who interprets omens, or a sorcerer. . ."* The Hebrew word

Thyatira

"sorcerer" used here in Deuteronomy 18:10 is the same Hebrew root word used for "witchcraft" to describe Jezebel in 2 Kings 9:22. Jezebel was a sorceress - a witch - according to the Law.

But there is another word in Deuteronomy 18:10 which is important, the word *"divination."* This word is found in 1 Samuel 15:23 where the Prophet Samuel told King Saul, *"For rebellion is as the sin of divination, and insubordination is as iniquity and idolatry."* This is the connection. The "witchcraft" of Jezebel and the "divination" of Saul were both forms of *spiritual rebellion* against God's authority. The sins of divination, witchcraft and rebellion all have a common root, namely, an improper relationship to God's power and authority. That is why divination and rebellion are linked. Jezebel was guilty of "witchcraft" which is spiritual rebellion, and Saul was guilty of rebellion which is spiritual divination. Witchcraft and divination are forms of rebellion, and rebellion is a form of witchcraft and divination. Both are the product of a wrong relationship to God's spiritual power and authority.

> *"The sins of divination, witchcraft and rebellion all have a common root, namely, an improper relationship to God's power and authority."*

The woman referred to as Jezebel in Thyatira claimed to be a prophetess (i.e., speaking for the Lord), but she walked in a spirit of witchcraft, divination and spiritual rebellion. By so doing she was exercising false spiritual authority over those around her. She exercised her false authority through false

When Jesus Visits His Church

teaching which led God's people astray (literally "causing them to wander," from Greek *planao* - "to wander"). *"This false Jezebel claimed to be a prophetess, having special revelations from God which qualified her to be an authoritative teacher."* [26] Thirty years earlier the Apostle Paul had used this same word to warn his young disciple Timothy, *"But the Spirit explicitly says that in later times some will fall away from the faith, paying attention to deceitful spirits and doctrines of demons . . ."* (1 Timothy 4:1) Paul warned Timothy that a time (literally, "a season") would come when people would fall away from the faith because they paid attention to the "deceitful" (*planos*) spirits of false teachers. For the believers in Thyatira, that season had now arrived.

> "She exercised her false authority through false teaching which led God's people astray."

Apparently this false prophetess taught the Christians of Thyatira that it was permissible for them to attend the guild meetings and to engage in the sexual immorality and idolatry which took place there. By means of her false teaching she was exercising false spiritual authority (i.e., "witchcraft") resulting in error, willful disobedience, immorality and idolatry.

---

[26] Ladd, page 51.

Thyatira

Five Lessons Regarding False Authority

I want to draw several quick lessons regarding false spiritual authority which are biblically and practically relevant:

Lesson # 1: God hates it when people exercise false or illegitimate spiritual authority over others. We see His attitude expressed in Jeremiah 5:30-31, *"An appalling and horrible thing has happened in the land: The prophets prophesy falsely, and the priests rule on their own authority; and My people love it so! But what will you do at the end of it?"* It is this hatred of false spiritual authority that brings about God's harsh treatment of false prophets, false shepherds and false teachers. Why? Because God understands "the end of it," namely, that false authority eventually leads to idolatry and "spiritual adultery."

Lesson # 2: God takes spiritual unfaithfulness seriously, so seriously that he describes it in terms of "spiritual adultery." In the Old Testament, "Spiritual adultery" and its consequences are at the heart of God's judgement expressed against His people in the book of Jeremiah. God views spiritual adultery (idolatry, false authority) with the same severity as He views literal unfaithfulness and adultery. You see, God understands something we don't. He understands *spiritual* unfaithfulness (described as "adultery") eventually leads to *literal* unfaithfulness (i.e., adultery and immorality).

Lesson # 3: God holds all people in positions of authority

When Jesus Visits His Church

accountable for what they teach and for any false authority they wield, because to God, false authority is equivalent to "witchcraft, sorcery and divination."

Lesson # 4: God is immensely and amazingly patient. This false prophetess in Thyatira had been given ample time (<u>chronos</u> - a measurable, chronological period of time) to repent, but she was unwilling.

Lesson # 5: While God is patient and gives people adequate time to repent, His longsuffering has limits. The opportunity for repentance is limited. So don't take it for granted or abuse it!

<u>'Here's What You Need To Do - Or Else'</u>

"Behold, I will cast her upon a bed of sickness, and those who commit adultery with her into great tribulation, unless they repent of her deeds. 'And I will kill her children with pestilence; and all the churches will know that I am He who searches the minds and hearts; and I will give to each one of you according to your deeds." (2:22-23)

The promise of the Risen Christ is that He will act against "Jezebel." One commentator (Farrer) has suggested that *"The punishment fits the crime - she who profaned the bed of love is pinned to the bed of sickness."* Others have suggested that the "bed" referred to was the couch on which one would recline at a meal, and still others have suggested that it is a funeral bier. Whatever the true meaning, the result

Thyatira

will be that both the false leader and her followers will experience "great tribulation" (or *"even greater pressure of crushing distress"*), unless they repent.

Repentance is the only way out of this situation. We should note that in a season of visitation God moves in power and holiness to judge both leaders and followers. Be careful how you lead, and be careful who you follow. During these seasons of visitation God also moves against false prophets, false prophecy and false authority. Why? So that *"all the churches will know"* His holiness and fear. God typically restores His authority over His Church by re-introducing wayward believers to His holiness. Why?

1. Because a holy Church is a fearful Church;
2. Because a fearful Church is a repentant Church;
3. Because a repentant Church is an intimate Church.

God acts so that His people can have confidence in Who He is, and that He deals with each of us *"according to your deeds."* In a very real sense, God wants a "fearful" church, because the "fear of God" is one of the greatest and most effective antidotes to false teachers, false teaching and false authority. As Martin Luther understood and demonstrated, the man who fears God doesn't fear other men.

<u>'Here's Something Else That I Noticed About You'</u>

"But I say to you, the rest who are in Thyatira, who do not hold this teaching, who have not known the deep things of

When Jesus Visits His Church

Satan, as they call them—I place no other burden on you. Nevertheless what you have, hold fast until I come." (2: 24-25)

The problem wasn't widespread among the people. The problem was limited to Jezebel, her followers and the church leadership who tolerated her activities. But the danger was that it would spread and become a scandal for the entire church if it remained unchecked. By the way, this admonition reminds us all to beware of false teachers who claim to be able to teach you "the really deep things of God." More often than not, their "deep things" have little or no depth, and little or nothing to do with God!

<u>'Just Between You And Me'</u>

"And he who overcomes, and he who keeps My deeds until the end, to him I will give authority over the nations; and he shall rule them with a rod of iron, as the vessels of the potter are broken to pieces, as I also have received authority from My Father; and I will give him the morning star." (2:26-28)

In His promised reward to the believers in Thyatira, the Risen Christ focuses upon something we might not expect - the willingness of the Christians in Thyatira to keep His "deeds." We have already seen (in the Church of Ephesus) that the Risen Christ uses the idea of "deeds" to refer to "faith." So, He may be admonishing the Christians in Thyatira to hold on to their faith and to remain faithful (unlike the false teacher Jezebel and her followers) "until the end." The "end" referred

Thyatira

to here is not the "End of the Age"(*sunteleia* - consumation). Rather it is the "completion" (Greek: *telos*) of the current series of trials they are experiencing, which will achieve their end or purpose either in victory or in death. The reward for their faithfulness-through-trials will be that Jesus will one day grant them authority to rule the nations, not in this present life and age, but in the Age to Come. This is consistent with Paul's admonishment to the Corinthian believers that they will one day "judge angels" (1 Corinthians 6:3).

<u>Do You Hear What I'm Saying?</u>

"He who has an ear, let him hear what the Spirit says to the churches." (2:29)

When Jesus Visits Your House Church

As you and your house church prepare a season of divine visitation, what can you learn from the Church of Thyatira? What do you hear the Holy Spirit saying to you and to the Church in your house through His message to the Church of Thyatira?

Fear, Awe and Authority - Is your church a "fearful" church, one that walks in genuine holiness and the fear of God? As we can see in Acts 5:11, God's holiness and fear tend to have the net effect of refocusing the attention of the Church back on God and His will and authority in our lives. Does Jesus have your full and undivided attention? When the Risen Christ visits your house church, whose authority will

When Jesus Visits His Church

He find you exercising or listening to? Do you understand and appreciate His authority over your life?

Jesus or Jezebel - Are you listening to a "Jezebel" who is using "the deep things of God" to exercise false authority over you and the Church? Be warned against such false teachers, lest you share in their judgment.

Authority, Witchcraft and Discernment - Do you know how to discern between false authority and true spiritual authority? If we are to be entrusted with authority over the nations, then we must learn the difference between true authority and false authority, between its proper and improper use. We all want authority because we assume we know how to wield it. That kind of assumption can quickly lead to witchcraft, divination and spiritual rebellion.

Repent! - Is it time for you to repent of having placed yourself under anyone's authority other than the authority of the Risen Christ?

Remember!
1. God's holiness leads to fear;
2. Fear leads to repentance;
3. Repentance leads to renewed intimacy with the Risen Christ!

Remember: *In the Kingdom of God, there is no prize for those who spiritually and morally compromise.*

Sardis

(Revelation 3:1-6)

"(1) And to the angel of the church in Sardis write: The words of him who has the seven spirits of God and the seven stars. 'I know your works. You have the reputation of being alive, but you are dead. (2) Wake up, and strengthen what remains and is about to die, for I have not found your works complete in the sight of my God. (3) Remember, then, what you received and heard. Keep it, and repent. If you will not wake up, I will come like a thief, and you will not know at what hour I will come against you. (4) Yet you have still a few names in Sardis, people who have not soiled their garments, and they will walk with me in white, for they are worthy. (5) The one who conquers will be clothed thus in white garments, and I will never blot his name out of the book of life. I will confess his name before my Father and before his angels. (6) He who has an ear, let him hear what the Spirit says to the churches."

When Jesus Visits His Church

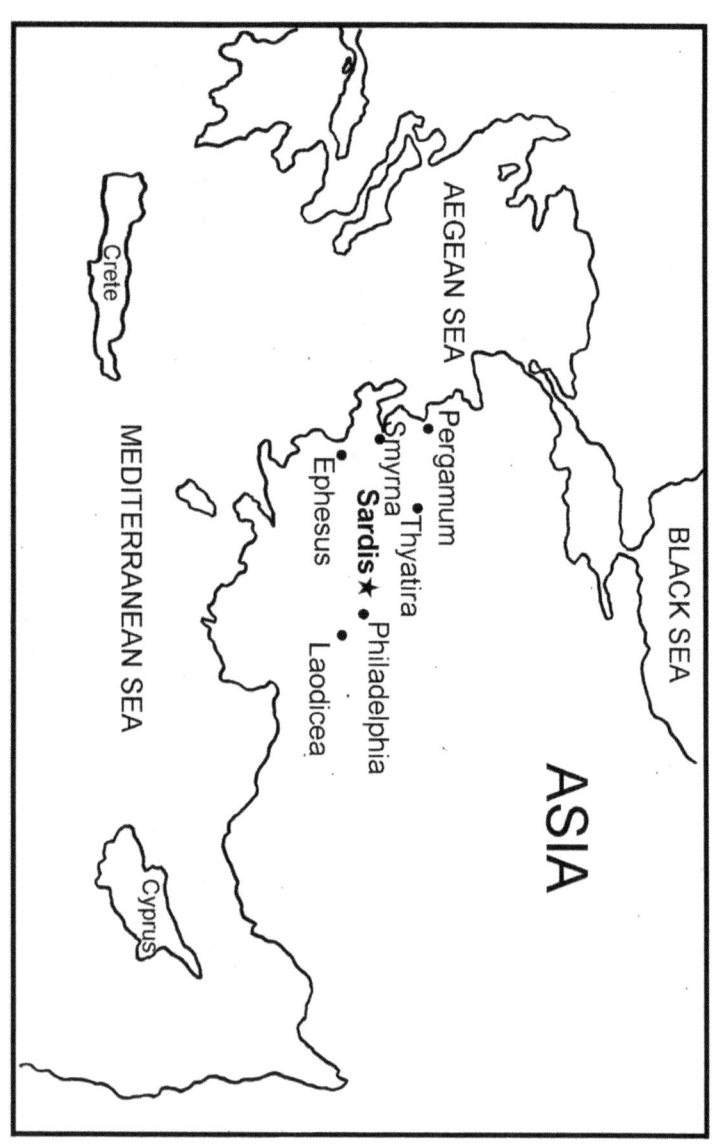

Sardis

*The Church That Fell Asleep
Living On Its Reputation
(Revelation 3:1-6)*

Background of Sardis

Sardis was a city 30 miles from Thyatira, situated on the mountain cliff of Timolus. Sardis was one of the famous cities of the ancient world. It was the capital and royal seat of the ancient Kingdom of Lydia and its most famous King, Croesus. In ancient times, Sardis was famed for its wealth, and for being impossible to conquer due to its location high upon a cliff. The nearby River Pactolus provided a generous source for gold and for the legendary wealth of the city. Gold and silver coins were first minted in the ancient work at Sardis. The glory days of Sardis, Lydia and Croesus came to an end when the city was conquered by the Persians in 549 B.C. The helmet of one of the defending soldiers fell down the cliff side. As he took an unknown path down to retrieve it, the enemies watched. Like "thieves in the night" they retraced his footsteps in single file and quietly entered the city. The sentries were surprised by the attack and the city fell without a fight. The city was conquered as it slept, by thieves in the night. They had become overly confident, and therefore, careless.

From that time onward the history of Sardis was the story of greatness in decline. Sardis eventually came under Roman rule in 133 B.C. In AD 26 when the cities of Asia contended for the honor of building the 2nd Asian temple to Rome and

When Jesus Visits His Church

the Emperor, the envoys from Sardis spoke long and eloquently about its past glory. Sardis, indeed, *"had a name, but was dead."* Unfortunately, the Christian community had become infected with the complacency of the place. Only a few had not "soiled their garments." Also, Sardis was home to an ancient Jewish colony which dated back to the Persian Era (547-344 B.C.). A large synagogue has been discovered that could have served a congregation of several thousand worshipers.

<u>*'Here's Who I Am In Relation To You'*</u>

"And to the angel of the church in Sardis write: He who has the seven Spirits of God, and the seven stars, says this . . ." (3:1a)

A Lesson About Lamps, Oil And Power

In order to fully understand how the Risen Christ is introducing himself to the Church at Sardis we need to do a couple of things. The first thing we need to do is to understand the imagery being used (lamps, spirits, lampstands, etc.). For example, Revelation 1:20 tells us that *"the seven lampstands are the Seven Churches."* In addition, Revelation 4:5 tells us that the seven "torches" (Greek: <u>*lampas*</u> - "lamps") are the seven spirits (i.e. spirits = lamps = churches). The diagram on the following page helps clarify some of these relationships.

Sardis

Based upon the imagery of the first two Chapters of Revelation, there is a close relationship between the "lamps," the "spirits" and the Churches. This leads us to the second thing we

> Lamps and Lampstands = Churches
>
> Lamps = Spirits = Churches
>
> Stars = Angels of Churches

need to understand in order to appreciate what the Risen Christ is communicating to the Church at Sardis. It is found in Old Testament book of Zechariah.

"And the angel who talked with me came again and woke me, like a man who is awakened out of his sleep. And he said to me, 'What do you see?' I said, 'I see, and behold, a lampstand all of gold, with a bowl on the top of it, and seven lamps on it, with seven lips on each of the lamps that are on the top of it. And there are two olive trees by it, one on the right of the bowl and the other on its left.' And I said to the angel who talked with me, 'What are these, my lord?' Then the angel who talked with me answered and said to me, 'Do you not know what these are?' I said, 'No, my lord.' Then he said to me, This is the word of the LORD to Zerubbabel: Not by might, nor by power, but by my Spirit, says the LORD of hosts." (Zechariah 4:1-6)

In this passage the Prophet Zechariah has a prophetic vision of a lampstand with seven lamps (basically a Jewish "menorah" or seven-branched lamp). The seven lamps are fed oil by two olive trees, one on each side. When it comes to symbols, types and figures in Scripture, oil is often

When Jesus Visits His Church

symbolic of the Holy Spirit. God's word to Zerubbabel is *"Not by might nor by power, but by My Spirit."* God's message to Zerubbabel is simple and clear: just as the lamps can't burn without oil, Zerubbabel can't do anything without the power of the Holy Spirit.

> *"Christ's word to the Church at Sardis is that they are a lampstand which can't do anything without the oil of the Holy Spirit. It is a word for the Church today, too!"*

What does this have to do with the Church at Sardis? Like their Old Testament counterparts, the lamps of the Book of Revelation are all lamps fed by oil. Without the oil of the Holy Spirit, they can shed no light. Christ's word to the Church at Sardis is that they are a lampstand which can't do anything without the oil of the Holy Spirit. It is a word for the Church today, too!

<u>*'Here's What I Know About What You've Been Doing'*</u>

"I know your works. You have the reputation of being alive, but you are dead."(3:1b)

Like the ancient city in which they now lived, the Church of Sardis had fallen into complacency - living on a reputation of former greatness which was no longer true. In spiritual terms, the Church of Sardis had become a lampstand with no oil which gave no light. Just as Sardis had a name and a reputation as a once-great city, but was now dead, so too,

Sardis

> "A reputation for being an organic house church is no substitute for the presence and power of the Holy Spirit!"

the Church of Sardis had a reputation as being a lampstand. But the Holy Spirit had departed, the oil was gone, and the light was extinguished. Like Moses wearing the veil over his face long after the glory of God had departed, there was no light in the Church of Sardis. For all practical purposes, they were spiritually dead. In the same way for us today, much of the organized visible church is living off the reputation and accumulated wealth of prior generations. We have a reputation of former greatness and influence, but little or no life so far as the world can see. A reputation, heritage or name is what a person, church or organization ends up with when the Holy Spirit departs. All that is left is a lamp without oil that gives no light. Does that describe your organic church today? A reputation for being an organic house church is no substitute for the presence and power of the Holy Spirit!

<u>*'Here's What You Need To Do - Or Else'*</u>

"Wake up, and strengthen what remains and is about to die, for I have not found your works complete in the sight of my God. Remember, then, what you received and heard. Keep it, and repent. If you will not wake up, I will come like a thief, and you will not know at what hour I will come against you." (3:2-3)

When Jesus Visits His Church

Five Commands

The Risen Christ challenges the Church of Sardis to examine its true spiritual condition by giving them five (5) specific commands, the most detailed instructions given to any of the Seven Churches.

Command # 1: "Wake up" - The command here isn't so much about waking up as it is about remaining watchful or alert. The Greek word <u>gregoreo</u> carries the idea of being vigilant or watchful. The meaning is that of *"vigilance and expectancy as contrasted with laxity and indifference."* The ancient defenders of Sardis had been conquered and defeated because they failed to be vigilant. The Christians of Sardis now ran the risk of being conquered rather than being "conquerors" due to their spiritual complacency. Like the believers in Sardis, it is time for the Church of th 21st Century to "wake up" and be "watchful and vigilant." It is time to "overcome."

"Spiritual complacency is so dangerous because it leads us and others into spiritual death!"

Command # 2: "Strengthen" - The Greek word <u>steridzo</u> means to turn resolutely in a certain direction, hence, to establish, to make firm or to strengthen something. It occurs 14 times in the N.T. In the letters of the Apostle Paul it is one of his favorite words for "establishing" believers in their faith He uses it 6 times. What were the believers in Smyrna to

Sardis

strengthen? The phrase *"the things that remain"* is a poor translation. The Greek word <u>loipos</u> means *"the rest"* and is frequently used of "other people" or "the remnant." Things don't die. People do. And there were believers in Sardis who needed to be established in their faith in order to survive. The Risen Christ commands the Church of Smyrna to strengthen and establish those other believers who were struggling with their spiritual condition and "were about to die." Spiritual complacency is so dangerous because it leads us and others into spiritual death!

Command # 3: "Remember" - The Scriptures have a lot to say about "remembering." The Greek word <u>mnemoneuo</u>, which occurs some 23 times in the N.T., suggests not simply remembering but "reflecting" on something. Earlier we saw how the Risen Christ admonished the believers in Ephesus to "remember" (same Greek word). Here the Risen Christ encourages the Christians in Sardis to remember and reflect on the truth of the Gospel which they had already received and heard. Sometimes we all need to stop, remember and reflect on the incredible truths which God has entrusted to us as disciples of His Kingdom.

Command # 4: "Keep" - The Greek word <u>tereo</u> means *"to watch over, to preserve, to keep or guard"* something. The idea here is *"to guard something from loss or injury by keeping an eye on it."* Not only were the believers of Sardis to remember and reflect on the truths of the Gospel they had already received, they were also to *"keep an eye on it and guard it against loss."* This is a warning against the danger of

When Jesus Visits His Church

complacency, the very problem which had caused the great city of Sardis to fall to its enemies. But it is also a call to faithfulness and perseverance, something we have already encountered in the Letters to the Seven Churches. It is a call for Christians to be vigilant in protecting and preserving the truths of the gospel. Protecting and preserving sound doctrine is important!

Command # 5: "Repent" - Does anyone not understand this? The believers in Sardis were going in the wrong direction. They were complacent and living off a reputation that no longer represented their true spiritual condition. The solution was for them to acknowledge their true spiritual condition, repent and go in a different direction.

There is a huge warning here. If the Christians of Sardis fail to keep these five commands, Jesus promises to come *"like a thief in the night"* just like the Persians had done nearly 600 years earlier. This is NOT a reference to an end-time "rapture." NO! This is God's judgment upon complacent Christians, living off their reputation of former greatness while failing to repent and be vigilant!

<u>'Here's Something Else I Noticed About You'</u>

"But you have a few people in Sardis who have not soiled their garments; and they will walk with Me in white; for they are worthy." (3:4)

Scripture emphasizes the importance of believers walking in

Sardis

a manner worthy of the Lord (See Ephesians 4:1; Colossians 1:10; 1 Thessalonians 2:2). To walk in a manner worthy of the Lord includes the idea of walking in "white," which is a symbol of moral and spiritual purity. The Greek word translated "soiled" is <u>moluno</u>. Since classical times it had meant "to stain, sully or defile," hence, "to disgrace oneself." Its use in Revelation 14:4 to describe those who had NOT "defiled themselves with women" suggests that John is using <u>moluno</u> to refer to sexual sin. In this context, to walk in "white" and in righteousness - to "walk in a manner worthy of the Lord" - includes a life of sexual and moral purity.

Revelation 19:8 says, *"And to her [the church] was granted that she should be arrayed in fine linen,* **clean and white***; for the fine linen is the righteousness of saints."* To walk in white garments is to walk in purity and righteousness. Garments of linen refer to the righteousness of the saints, while defiled garments refer to unrighteousness. To walk in righteousness is to be right with God as accomplished through he sacrificial death of Christ on our behalf. As Paul says, *"For our sake he made him to be sin who knew no sin, so that in him we might become the righteousness of God."* (2 Corinthians 5:21) But to walk in righteousness - in a manner worthy of the Lord - is also to walk in personal holiness as an outward expression of that inward reality.

<u>'Just Between You and Me'</u>

"The one who conquers will be clothed thus in white garments, and I will never blot his name out of the book of

When Jesus Visits His Church

life. I will confess his name before my Father and before his angels." (3:5)

The reward of the Risen Christ to the faithful believers in Sardis continues the idea of purity, namely, they will be *"clothed in white garments."* The faithful believers in Sardis will walk with Christ in unsoiled, white garments of righteousness.

But there is more. In John's day, the king of any land always kept a register that was very much like a census. If a person committed a crime against the state, his name was removed from the register and he was no longer considered a citizen. The king also kept a register of the living subjects of his kingdom who had not rebelled against him. Here Jesus promises the faithful believers of Thyatira that he will NOT blot their names out of His Kingly register, but will acknowledge them before the Father, just as He promised in Matthew 10:32-33. *"As a civic register contained the names of living citizens, so God's book of life contains the names of the Saints. The form of the promise in the present passage is an assurance of salvation in the consummated Kingdom of God."*[27]

Jesus' words here are a warning to all of us. A lack of personal vigilance, combined with the complacency of living on our reputation and a refusal to obey Christ's commands,

---

[27]Ladd, ***A Commentary On The Revelation Of John***, page 57-58.

Sardis

constitute a form of denying Christ (which is the context of Matthew 10:32-33). This is not about the possibility of losing one's salvation. It is about the spiritual self-examination every believer needs to practice to assure that our own profession of faith is genuine, as reflected in our obedience, and that our names are, indeed, written in the book of life when Judgment Day arrives.

<u>'Do You Hear What I'm Saying?'</u>

"He who has an ear, let him hear what the Spirit says to the churches." (3:6)

When Jesus Visits Your House Church

As you and your house church prepare for a season of divine visitation, what can you learn from the Church of Sardis? What do you hear the Holy Spirit saying to you and to the Church in your house through His message to the Church of Sardis?

The Past vs The Future - Are you living off of a reputation that is no longer descriptive of your true spiritual condition? If so, what do you intend to do about it, starting today?

Reality vs Fantasy - What is your true spiritual condition? Have you and your house church become a "lamp with no oil"? Is it time for you to "take stock" of spiritual reality in your life and repent?

When Jesus Visits His Church

Complacency vs Vigilance - Like the believers of Sardis, you and I have a need for constant vigilance and watchfulness regarding the spiritual condition of our lives. The antidote to spiritual complacency is found in obeying the five commands of the Risen Christ:

> Command # 1: "Wake up"
> Command # 2: "Strengthen"
> Command # 3: "Remember"
> Command # 4: "Keep"
> Command # 5: "Repent"

Remember: *In the Kingdom of God, there is no prize for those who spiritually and morally compromise.*

Philadelphia
(Revelation 3:7-13)

"(7) And to the angel of the church in Philadelphia write: The words of the holy one, the true one, who has the key of David, who opens and no one will shut, who shuts and no one opens. (8) 'I know your works. Behold, I have set before you an open door, which no one is able to shut. I know that you have but little power, and yet you have kept my word and have not denied my name. (9) Behold, I will make those of the synagogue of Satan who say that they are Jews and are not, but lie—behold, I will make them come and bow down before your feet, and they will learn that I have loved you. (10) Because you have kept my word about patient endurance, I will keep you from the hour of trial that is coming on the whole world, to try those who dwell on the earth. (11) I am coming soon. Hold fast what you have, so that no one may seize your crown. (12) The one who conquers, I will make him a pillar in the temple of my God. Never shall he go out of it, and I will write on him the name of my God, and the name of the city of my God, the new Jerusalem, which comes down from my God out of heaven, and my own new name. (13) He who has an ear, let him hear what the Spirit says to the churches."

When Jesus Visits His Church

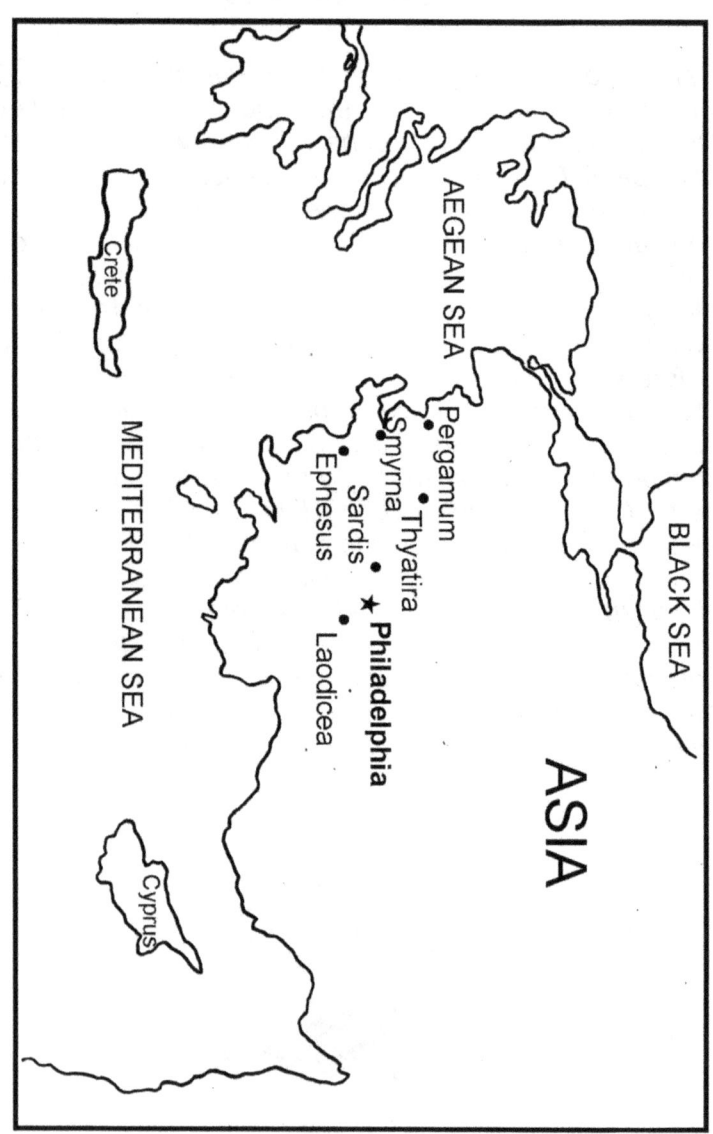

Philadelphia

*The Church Which Held Fast
and Was Vindicated
(Revelation 3:7-13)*

The Opening and Closing of Doors

Perhaps you already know the story of Trans World Radio (TRW), founded in 1952 as a ministry for the mass communication of the good news of Jesus Christ. Burdened for the people of Spain, TWR founder Dr. Paul E. Freed realized that radio would be the ideal vehicle to reach those in that spiritually needy land. He discovered an open door to establish a missionary radio station in Tangier, Morocco, directly across the Strait of Gibraltar from Spain.

The first "Voice of Tangier" broadcast aired over a 2,500-watt transmitter on February 22, 1954. Programming began in two languages (Spanish and English), and by January of 1956 the station was broadcasting to 40 countries in more than 20 languages. Then, the Moroccan government announced that all radio installations were to be nationalized as of December 31, 1959. Dr. Freed had already begun negotiating with Radio Monte Carlo in Monaco with the view of moving the ministry from Morocco (in Africa) to the European continent. God opened a door, and in 1960, TWR moved across the Strait of Gibraltar to Monte Carlo.

In a divine irony that only God could have arranged, Trans World Radio began broadcasting the good news of the

When Jesus Visits His Church

Kingdom of God from a station originally constructed by Adolph Hitler to proclaim his victory over Europe and to air Nazi propaganda throughout Europe during World War II. Funny thing about doors. Often times it is men who build them, but God Who uses them.

Background of Philadelphia

The Asian city of Philadelphia was originally founded in 189 B.C. by Attalus, the King of Pergamum, who built it in memory of his brother. Attalus founded it with the specific intention of making it a "missionary center" from which to spread Greek language, culture and civilization to all the region east of Philadelphia. The city stood at a point where three Asian provinces converged - Lydia, Mysia and Phrygia. Situated on the major highway between east and west Asia, it commanded an important mountain pass between the Hermus and Meander valleys. It was literally the "doorway" through which passed the mail, trade and commerce of the west on its way to the regions east. It became the gateway, the 'open door,' to the Exotic East as far as the West was concerned. Down the main streets of the city stood a series of pillars engraved with the names of eminent citizens along with the name of Emperor who honored them for their great services, followed by the name of the city and then the name of the citizen who is honored. Often he was given a new title. In addition it was customary in Philadelphia to honor men who had served the city with distinction. A pillar would be erected in one of the city's temples. On it was inscribed the person's name, the name of the city where he was born, and

Philadelphia

the name of the god he held in highest reverence.

Philadelphia was also situated on a major geological fault line in an active volcanic zone which meant it was always under constant threat of destruction. Its soil was black soil, which was ideal for growing grapes - a contribution of the volcanic mountains. As a result, its major exports were wine and the religion of the wine god, Dionysius. The city was wealthy and excavations indicate that the houses in the city had running hot and cold water. The hot water was piped from hot water springs which abounded in the volcanic mountain area. The Roman historian, Tacitus, lists Philadelphia third among the cities of Asia which received earthquake relief from the Roman Senate following the great earthquake of AD 17. The city briefly changed its name as an expression of gratitude for the relief given by Rome. Its new name, "Neocaesarea" ("Caesar's New City") appeared briefly on coinage, but did not last.

It is believed that Christians came to this area in a humanitarian mission to help the victims of volcanic destruction and won the city. The city experienced frequent earth tremors, causing its population to go out to the open country to escape the danger of falling walls. The walls of excavated houses are cracked, bearing the marks of frequent earthquakes. Philadelphia was also home to an active synagogue of Jews which actively sought to persecute the church there, and which the Risen Christ describes as a "Synagogue of Satan."

When Jesus Visits His Church

<u>*'Here's Who I Am In Relation To You'*</u>

"And to the angel of the church in Philadelphia write: The words of the holy one, the true one, who has the key of David, who opens and no one will shut, who shuts and no one opens." (3:7)

The Risen Christ introduces Himself in terms the Christians of Philadelphia would understand - as the one who opens and closes doors. He quotes from Isaiah 22 where God raises up Eliakim as a faithful steward to replace Shebna, an unfaithful steward, in the household of King Hezekiah:

"I will thrust you from your office, and you will be pulled down from your station. In that day I will call my servant Eliakim the son of Hilkiah, and I will clothe him with your robe, and will bind your sash on him, and will commit your authority to his hand. And he shall be a father to the inhabitants of Jerusalem and to the house of Judah. And I will place on his shoulder the key of the house of David. He shall open, and none shall shut; and he shall shut, and none shall open. And I will fasten him like a peg in a secure place, and he will become a throne of honor to his father's house." (Isaiah 22:19-23)

In Isaiah's day this passage was also a prophecy about a Coming One who would become "a throne of glory." Jesus was that prophesied one, and He now has the key and is able to open and close what men cannot.

Philadelphia

Ladd summarizes John's point this way,

"The key of David is the key to David's house - the messianic Kingdom. The immediate background of the phrase was the claim of the Jews in Philadelphia that they were the true people of God who held the key to the Kingdom of God. John contradicts this claim by asserting that the key to the Kingdom which had belonged to Israel really belongs to Jesus as the Davidic Messiah (5:5; 2:16) and had been forfeited by Israel because she had rejected her Messiah." [28]

<u>'Here's What I Know About What You've Been Doing'</u>

"I know your works. Behold, I have set before you an open door, which no one is able to shut. I know that you have but little power, and yet you have kept my word and have not denied my name. Behold, I will make those of the synagogue of Satan who say that they are Jews and are not, but lie—behold, I will make them come and bow down before your feet, and they will learn that I have loved you." (3:8-9)

An Open Door

According to verse 8, the Risen Christ is placing before the Philadelphian believers an open door. He gives three reasons why He is giving these believers an open door:

Reason # 1: Powerlessness - Because they have "a little

---

[28]Ladd, ***A Commentary On The Revelation Of John***, page 59.

When Jesus Visits His Church

power." The Greek word for "little" (*micron*) is the word which we use to describe things so small that they are "microscopic." The open door God places before His people does not depend upon their power, but upon His. The issue is God's power to open doors, not our power to open them ourselves. God does great things through people who understand that they have little power, but He does little through those who think that they have great power.

> "God does great things through people who understand that they have little power, but He does little through those who think that they have great power."

Reason # 2: Perseverance - Because they have "kept My word." The Greek word (*tereo*) means to watch over, to preserve, to keep or guard something. It occurs 5 times in the seven letters - 2:26; 3:3; 3:8; 3:10 (2X) Jesus always commends those who keep what He has entrusted to them. In this situation their actions demonstrate perseverance. We know this from verse 10 where the same commendation appears in a slightly different form: *"Because you have kept the word of My perseverance."* God honors perseverance in our lives.

> "A little power with perseverance and faithfulness is better in God's sight than great power with little or no perseverance or faithfulness."

Philadelphia

A little power with perseverance and faithfulness is better in God's sight than great power with little or no perseverance or faithfulness.

Reason # 3: Faithfulness - Faithfulness is important to God. The point of the story about Shebna and Eliakim is that God was punishing the unfaithfulness of Shebna and rewarding the faithfulness of Eliakim. The same is now true regarding the faithfulness of the believers in Philadelphia, because they "have not denied My Name." Denying Christ's Name is a "big deal" in the New Testament: *"Everyone therefore who shall confess Me before men, I will also confess him before My Father who is in heaven. But whoever shall deny Me before men, I will also deny him before My Father who is in heaven."* (Matthew 10:32-33) The refusal of these believers to deny Christ's name was a sign of their faithfulness . . . and their perseverance.

Vindication - The Risen Christ promises to vindicate His Church against the "Synagogue of Satan" by causing them *"to come and bow down at your feet."* Vindication is always about God vindicating Himself and His call upon us. Vindication is God judging and distinguishing between that which is of Him and that which is not. This idea of vindication as judgment is most clearly seen in the Old Testament where the Hebrew word for "vindicate" also means "to judge."

<u>'Here's Something Else That I Noticed About You'</u>

"Because you have kept my word about patient endurance,

When Jesus Visits His Church

I will keep you from the hour of trial that is coming on the whole world, to try those who dwell on the earth. I am coming soon. Hold fast what you have, so that no one may seize your crown." (3:10-11)

"My Word About Patient Endurance" - There are times in the life of the individual believer and the Church when our faithfulness to Christ and our refusal to compromise our faith requires "patient endurance" - perseverance. Perseverance in the face of persecution and the overwhelming pressure to compromise our faith is something the Risen Christ notices and rewards.

As we have already learned in the introduction, "patient endurance" or "perseverance" is one of the three things which the Apostle John sees believers sharing in together. The believers in Philadelphia had taken seriously - held onto - Jesus' word concerning the importance of perseverance. As the ESV translates it, *"Because you have kept my word about patient endurance."*

"The Hour of Testing" - The primary meaning of *peirasmos* is not "temptation," as some translations render it, but "testing," that is *"proving, assaying, testing"* in order to determine quality, such as metals tested by fire. By their perseverance and faithfulness the Philadelphian believers had already "proven their metal" - the quality of their faith - so that no further testing was needed. The next 200 years did indeed become an "hour of testing" for the Church throughout the Roman Empire (the Roman Empire was

Philadelphia

frequently regarded as constituting "the inhabited earth"). Like precious metal tested by fire, every season of persecution represents an hour of testing during which God tests and proves the quality of believers' faith.[29]

"Hold Fast" - The primary meaning of <u>krateo</u> is *"to use strength to seize or retain something,"* hence, to hold fast. It is used six times in the seven letters to encourage believers to be faithful and NOT compromise their faith. God always blesses those who "hold fast" their faith when confronted with the crushing pressure of circumstances and the overwhelming temptation to compromise.

"Let No One Take Your Crown" - There are several places in the New Testament where believers are promised crowns (see 1 Corinthians 9:25; 2 Timothy 4:8; James 1:12; 1 Peter 5:4; Revelation 2:10 and 3:11). Consider Paul's words in 1 Corinthians 9:24-25 when he says:

"Do you not know that in a race all the runners run, but only one receives the prize? So run that you may obtain it. Every athlete exercises self-control in all things. They do it to receive a perishable wreath, but we an imperishable."

Question: How can someone take your prize? How can they

---

[29] Ladd points out, *"Here is a distinct eschatological reference to the 'messianic woes' which are to precede the return of the Lord. John viewed the troubles which the church will suffer in the near future against the background of the consummation of evil and the time of terrible trouble at the end."* Ladd, page 62.

When Jesus Visits His Church

take your crown?
Answer: By beating you in the race.

Question: How can they beat you in the race?
Answer: By encouraging you to compromise your faith.

Question: Are you racing to win? Because that's what it takes to possess the crown.

<u>'Just Between You And Me'</u>

"The one who conquers, I will make him a pillar in the temple of my God. Never shall he go out of it, and I will write on him the name of my God, and the name of the city of my God, the new Jerusalem, which comes down from my God out of heaven, and my own new name." (3:12)

The Christians of Philadelphia were a small group with very little power. But the Risen Christ comforts and encourages them by promising that the honor He will bestow upon them will be far greater than the inscriptions on the pillars of the city which honor men for their public service. And while local pagan officials might honor men with temporary pillars in the local temples, faithful believers in Jesus will become pillars in God's temple which will stand eternally.

The danger confronting and challenging the Church in every age is the temptation to "pander to power" and to compromise its beliefs and its witness for the sake of achieving acceptance and approval.

Philadelphia

'Do You Hear What I'm Saying?'

"He who has an ear, let him hear what the Spirit says to the churches." (3:13)

When Jesus Visits Your House Church

As you and your house church prepare for a season of divine visitation, what can you learn from the Church of Philadelphia? What do you hear the Holy Spirit saying to you and to the Church in your house through His message to the Church of Philadelphia?

Powerlessness - The Risen Christ placed an open door before the believers of Philadelphia because their powerlessness would allow God to show Himself powerful on their behalf. What open door is God placing before you? Are you willing to admit your own powerlessness and allow God to show Himself powerful on your behalf?

Perseverance - Because the believers in Philadelphia had persevered, Jesus was going to spare them from "the hour of testing." Perseverance in the things of God brings its own reward when others are being judged or tested. How are you persevering in the things of God?

Faithfulness - How are you being faithful to the name of Christ in the face of opposition, persecution and the ongoing pressure to compromise your faith?

When Jesus Visits His Church

Hold Fast - Are you holding fast to your faith and to the truths you have received and known over the years as a believer in the face of an increasingly hostile world?

Let No One Take Your Crown - How well are you running and competing in the "race of faith." Are you in danger of someone "taking your crown" because you are not running well?

Remember: *In the Kingdom of God, there is no prize for those who spiritually and morally compromise.*

Laodicea

(Revelation 3:14-22)

"(14) And to the angel of the church in Laodicea write: The words of the Amen, the faithful and true witness, the beginning of God's creation. (15) 'I know your works: you are neither cold nor hot. Would that you were either cold or hot! (16) So, because you are lukewarm, and neither hot nor cold, I will spit you out of my mouth. (17) For you say, I am rich, I have prospered, and I need nothing, not realizing that you are wretched, pitiable, poor, blind, and naked. (18) I counsel you to buy from me gold refined by fire, so that you may be rich, and white garments so that you may clothe yourself and the shame of your nakedness may not be seen, and salve to anoint your eyes, so that you may see. (19) Those whom I love, I reprove and discipline, so be zealous and repent. (20) Behold, I stand at the door and knock. If anyone hears my voice and opens the door, I will come in to him and eat with him, and he with me. (21) The one who conquers, I will grant him to sit with me on my throne, as I also conquered and sat down with my Father on his throne. (22) He who has an ear, let him hear what the Spirit says to the churches."

When Jesus Visits His Church

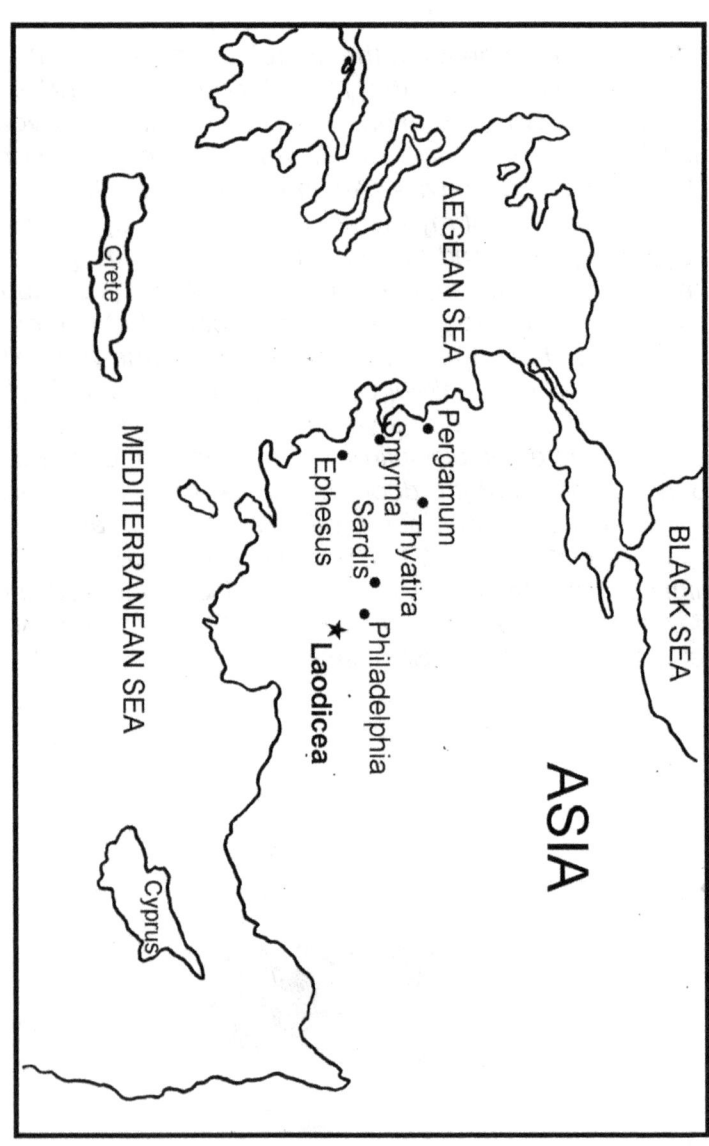

Laodicea

*A Lukewarm Church of
Personal Peace and Affluence
(Revelation 3:14-22)*

There I sat at a local Starbucks, trying desperately to write and mind my own business for a few quiet moments. But it wasn't working. My eye kept being drawn toward the person next to me and the book he was reading - a best-selling motivational book by a mega-church pastor out of Houston, Texas. Finally, I could no longer resist and I introduced myself and asked how he was enjoying it. He was profuse in his praise for the book. I asked him about his line of work. He and his wife were independent business people in a wonderful business opportunity . . . which being interpreted from the common Greek came to mean multi-level marketing. Determined to short-circuit the inevitable presentation I gave him my card and invited him and his wife to visit our Friday night house church gathering (which he expressed interest in attending, but alas . . .).

Our conversation tapered off, and after he left I sat there marveling at the fulfillment of prophecy, namely, the prophecy given some 30 years ago by Dr. Francis A. Schaeffer. In his landmark work, ***How Should We Then Live?*** Dr. Schaeffer wrote that the church of the late 20th Century stood on the verge of adopting what he called the "two terrible values" of "personal peace" and "personal affluence." Personal peace meant "leave me alone," while personal affluence meant "leave me alone with my affluent

When Jesus Visits His Church

lifestyle and all my affluent toys." Thirty years later in a Starbucks, there I sat realizing the extent to which his prophetic words had been fulfilled. Today we live in an age of Christian entitlement and consumerism, the very embodiment of Dr. Schaeffer's personal peace and personal affluence, complete with books, seminars and TV preachers ready to convince us that those two terrible values are, in reality-and-truth-of-fact, spiritual virtues, the very will and plan of God for your life and mine.

A survey of college students in the 1970s (when Dr. Schaeffer was active) revealed that the goal of the average college student was to find a philosophy of life. The same survey today reveals that the goal of the average college student is to make money. Apparently, in the thirty years since Dr. Schaeffer, college students have found their philosophy of life; it's called "materialism" and expresses itself as the pursuit of personal peace and personal affluence . . . even at Church!

No, I'm not wandering off track here. Because the Church of the 21st Century is, in reality, suffering from the same malady which afflicted the Church of Laodicea nearly 2000 years ago - a lukewarm complacency born out of personal peace and personal affluence. And therein lies a story and a message.

Background of Laodicea

In Roman times (from 133 B.C. onwards) the town of Laodicea was both a military outpost and a trade center. The

Laodicea

town of Laodicea was situated east of Ephesus and was one of a group of three towns which lay within easy sight of each other at a point where the narrow glen of the river Lycus broadens out into the lower valley. The other two towns were Hierapolis and Colossae (Paul refers to Laodicea and Hierapolis in Colossians 4:13).

Laodicea was a wealthy trading center. Of the Seven Churches addressed by John in Revelation 2-3, Laodicea was the richest of the seven, becoming affluent and widely known as a banking center where the business of "money changing" flourished. It was the banking center for the whole of Asia Minor, even minting its own coins. The Roman orator Cicero cashed his letters of credit there.

When the city was heavily damaged by an earthquake in AD 60, Rome offered her the same grants and tax relief for rebuilding that Sardis and Philadelphia had been given. But Laodicea refused the help, preferring to rebuild out of its own resources *"with no help from us,"* as the Roman historian Tacitus noted.

Laodicea was also famous for its black sheep which produced a highly sought after wool that was woven locally into fabric and garments. Like Pergamum, Laodicea also boasted a medical school and produced an opium-based poultice for treating eye ailments which was regarded by the ancients as a miracle remedy. The Apostle Paul encouraged the Church at Colossae to read his letter to the Church at Laodicea (See Colossians 4:16. This letter of Paul to

When Jesus Visits His Church

Laodicea has not survived), and to circulate the letter he wrote to Colossae to the Laodiceans.

'Here's Who I Am In Relation To You'

"And to the angel of the church in Laodicea write: The words of the Amen, the faithful and true witness, the beginning of God's creation. (3:14)

The Risen Christ is about to bear faithful witness and to speak truth to the slumbering, lukewarm believers of Laodicea, so He introduces Himself as *"the faithful and true Witness"* (see also Revelation 1:5). He is about to bear faithful witness and confirm their true spiritual condition. And it is going to come as something of a shock to a church that was living in comfortable, affluent denial.

Here's What I Know About What You've Been Doing

"I know your works: you are neither cold nor hot. Would that you were either cold or hot! So, because you are lukewarm, and neither hot nor cold, I will spit you out of my mouth." (3:15-16)

Your Apathy Makes Me Sick

Like the other six (6) Churches of Asia, the Church of Laodicea had "deeds," and Jesus knew it. They were busy "doing the works," but unfortunately these were the deeds of a lukewarm, tepid people. Theirs were the works of apathy.

Laodicea

"The trouble at Laodicea was that the church members were neither hot nor cold. They were not characterized by the coldness of hostility to the gospel or rejection of the faith; but neither were they characterized by a warm zeal and fervor (Acts 18:25; Romans 11:11). They were simply indifferent, nominal, complacent."[30]

Jesus' response was that their lukewarmness nauseated Him, and He was going to vomit them out of His mouth (yep, that's what it says, even in the Greek!).

"For you say, I am rich, I have prospered, and I need nothing, not realizing that you are wretched, pitiable, poor, blind, and naked." (3:17)

You Are Living A Delusion of Self-Sufficiency

This verse creates a contrast between the Laodiceans' physical condition as they saw and understood it, and their true spiritual condition as the Risen Christ saw it. Outwardly and physically, they gave every appearance of having it all together. By all outward measurements they were indeed rich, wealthy and in need of nothing (literally *"to have need for not one thing"*). But spiritually this Church was serious trouble. *"No doubt part of her problem was the inability to distinguish between material and spiritual prosperity. The church that is prospering materially and outwardly can easily fall into the self-deception that her outward prosperity is the*

---

[30]Ladd, ***A Commentary On The Revelation Of John***, page 65.

When Jesus Visits His Church

measure of her spiritual prosperity." [31]

The Laodicean believers lacked zeal and vision for the things of God. Spiritually speaking they were blind to their condition, unable to see that they were really suffering spiritual hardship, that they were spiritually miserable, and that they had been reduced to the status of desperate spiritual beggars. All of this would have come as news to the believers of Laodicea - just as it would come as news to many believers today.

The idea communicated by the Greek here is mendicancy, "public paupers." In spiritual terms, they had been reduced to begging on the streets for

> *"The Laodicean believers lacked zeal and vision for the things of God."*

their daily needs. In spite of the famous Laodicean eye salve which was in great demand, they were themselves spiritually blind and unable to see. And in spite of their famous black wool (from which clothes would be made) they were spiritually naked in God's sight and in need of new clothes. They might be physically well off, but they were spiritually destitute.

Like the ancient Laodiceans of John's day, most Western believers live in a physical and economic affluence that is at least equivalent to that of the Laodiceans (probably much

---

[31] Ladd, page 66.

Laodicea

greater!). And like the Laodiceans we need to ask ourselves if we are as wealthy inwardly and spiritually as we are outwardly and physically.

Twenty five years ago Dr. Francis Schaeffer declared that one of the greatest dangers facing the Church was what he called the two terrible values of "Personal Peace" and "Personal Affluence." These two terrible values, he said, would manifest themselves in an attitude which said, *"Leave me alone with my possessions and my affluence, and I don't care what else happens."* Isn't this the false, self-sufficient and complacent spirit of the Laodiceans? And isn't this the attitude of much of the Church today?

> "Money can't buy what we truly need and what only God can give."

<u>'Here's What You Need To Do - Or Else'</u>

"I counsel you to buy from me gold refined by fire, so that you may be rich, and white garments so that you may clothe yourself and the shame of your nakedness may not be seen, and salve to anoint your eyes, so that you may see." (3:18)

Let Me Give You Some Advice

It is significant that Jesus here offers advice, but He does not command (although when the risen Son of God gives advice, it is probably a good idea to listen and obey!). Here Jesus offers a different kind of gold. The gold coinage of Laodicea

When Jesus Visits His Church

was insufficient to buy what they needed. Money can't buy what we truly need and what only God can give. They needed a different kind of gold in order to buy what Jesus was offering. And gold couldn't buy the type of clothing which the Laodiceans needed in order to cover their spiritual nakedness. Laodicea was famous for producing black wool and exquisite garments, but here Christ offers them "white garments." What are these, and what is the nakedness that needs to be covered? Perhaps these are the robes of Christ's righteousness and sufficiency given to cover the nakedness of their spiritual poverty and self-righteousness and self-sufficiency. And the Laodiceans could neither produce nor buy the kind of eye ointment needed to heal their spiritual blindness. But the risen Christ offers them a different kind of eye salve, in contrast with what Laodicea was famous for. His salve will heal their spiritual eyes so they can see both their true spiritual condition and the abundant provision Jesus has available to give them. Jesus appears to be saying, *"You need nothing you already have, but you need everything that I have."*

If I Didn't Love You, I Wouldn't Say This

*'Those whom I love, I reprove and discipline; be zealous therefore, and **repent.**"* (3:19)

Jesus now moves from giving advice to specific admonishments and commands. The word "discipline" (Greek: _paideuo_) here means *"to raise as a child."* The language of this passage echoes the more extensive

Laodicea

language of Hebrews Chapter 12:6ff and the importance of discipline (i.e., "chastisement") in producing maturity and holiness in the life of the believer. Here Jesus reaffirms His love for them, while admonishing the Laodiceans as children. There are two commands here:

Command # 1: Be Zealous! - The first command to the believers of Laodicea is that they should "be zealous" as opposed to being lukewarm and complacent. What exactly does it mean to be "zealous"? The answer to that question requires some explaining. In first century

> *"It was time for the Laodiceans to "get radical" about Jesus!"*

Judaism there existed a group of people know as "the Zealots." These were radical Jews who sought to incite the people of Judah to rebel against the Roman Empire and expel it from Palestine by force. According to Josephus, the Zealots *"agree in all other things with the Pharisaic notions; but they have an inviolable attachment to liberty, and say that God is to be their only Ruler and Lord."* (Josephus, Antiquities, 18.1.6) The Zealots opposed Roman rule by targeting Romans and Greeks for assassination. The Zealots were instrumental in the Jewish Revolt of A.D. 66. They seized Jerusalem and held it until 70, when the son of Roman Emperor Vespasian, Titus, retook the city and destroyed Herod's Temple. Jesus had a disciple who, apparently, was a Zealot. The Jewish Zealots of the first century embodied a radical commitment to and jealousy for God and Jewish nationalism. It was misplaced, but it was

When Jesus Visits His Church

genuine. This is the background that would have colored any first-century reader of this letter to the Church of Laodicea. The Risen Christ is telling the lukewarm believers of Laodicea that they need to be as "zealous" for the things of God as the original political zealots were for their misplaced ideology. It was time for the Laodiceans to "get radical" about Jesus!

Command # 2: Repent! - The second command is that they should "repent." Simply put, they needed to recognize and acknowledge their true condition and change the way they think about themselves and the way they go about their lives. It was time to think and act differently.

"Behold, I stand at the door and knock. If anyone hears my voice and opens the door, I will come in to him and eat with him, and he with me." (3:20)

This Knock-Knock Is No Joke

An "Inside-Out Church" - The command to repent is followed by an offer of intimacy with the Risen Christ. Intimacy with Jesus is always available to the repentant believer. But look at the word picture. Where is Christ? He is on the outside of His own church! This verse is often mis-used

> *"Jesus is knocking on the door of His own church seeking to gain entry. From His perspective, Jesus wasn't even part of the Laodicean Church."*

Laodicea

to describe Jesus as knocking on the door of an unbeliever's heart and wanting to come into their life. But that is not the context of this verse. What's happening here is quite different. Jesus is knocking on the door of His own church seeking to gain entry. From His perspective, Jesus wasn't even part of the Laodicean Church. He was on the outside looking in! Someone has suggested that Jesus is standing as the master of the house, knocking on the door and expecting alert servants to respond and welcome His coming. If Jesus is indeed knocking on the door of the Church today in a season of divine visitation, where are the alert bond-servants of the King who will respond in repentance and faith and welcome His coming?!

Maybe it is time for us to pause and to ask ourselves, *How did this happen?! How did Jesus end up on the outside of His own Church?!* And how often is that true of churches today? How often are they pursuing their own agendas and programs, oblivious to the reality that Jesus is outside - a stranger to His own Church and seeking entry. Genuine repentance appears to be a pre-requisite for restoring intimacy with God, either as individuals or as a corporate body. Genuine repentance is our way of inviting Jesus to retake His rightful position as "master of the house," both in our personal lives and in His Church, including your house church.

<u>'Just Between You And Me'</u>

"The one who conquers, I will grant him to sit with me on my

When Jesus Visits His Church

throne, as I also conquered and sat down with my Father on his throne." (3:21)

This is a reward worthy of all our zeal: the unspeakable honor of sitting down with Jesus on His throne! But it is not a reward that will be given to the tepid and lukewarm believers of Laodicea unless, and until, they repent!

'Do You Hear What I'm Saying?'

'He who has an ear, let him hear what the Spirit says to the churches.'" (3:21-22)

When Jesus Visits Your House Church

As you and your house church prepare for a season of divine visitation, what can you learn from the Church of Laodicea? What do you hear the Holy Spirit saying to you and to the Church in your house through His message to the Church of Laodicea?

If Jesus, the Risen Christ, were to visit your house church today, just as He promised to visit the Seven Churches of Asia, what would he find?

Hot, Cold or Lukewarm? - Which are you? It is a spiritual reality that lukewarm, tepid people will never overcome and conquer the spiritual battles we are facing as individuals or as a Church. Something must change. And something will change when Jesus visits His church! We need to repent of

Laodicea

our lukewarm attitudes toward the things of God, and at the same time we need to pray that the Holy Spirit would grant us a renewed zeal!

Rich but Poor - The Laodiceans were materially affluent, but spiritually they were poverty-stricken. Their material prosperity had lulled them to sleep. And like the believers in Sardis, the Laodicean believers were unaware of their true spiritual condition. How about you? What is your spiritual condition? We need to repent for attitudes of personal peace and personal affluence that have caused us to become materially wealthy but spiritually destitute. At the same time we need to repent for failing to recognize and confess our true spiritual condition.

Reproof And Discipline - Like the Laodiceans, do we fail to understand or appreciate that sometimes Jesus expresses His love for us through reproof and discipline (chastisement). We need to repent for refusing to recognize and accept the discipline of the Lord in our lives, rather than blaming it on the Enemy and doing pointless warfare against it.

Remember: *In the Kingdom of God, there is no prize for those who spiritually and morally compromise.*

When Jesus Visits His Church

Epilogue

A Time To Reflect

It is now time to end this study with the same question with which we began this study: If Jesus were to visit your house church the same way He promised to visit the house churches in Asia Minor in Revelation Chapters 2 and 3, what would He find and what would He say?

In our journey through the Seven Churches of Asia Minor we have discovered many lessons we can all meditate on, lessons about lost love, persecution, false teachers and false authority, complacency and lukewarmness, open doors and the importance of perseverance and faithfulness. I will leave it to you to reflect on those lessons and what they mean to you and your house church. I want to offer a few closing observations on what I see as the over-arching theme of the Seven Letters, namely, compromise.

The Challenge of Compromise

The challenge for biblical Christians and disciples of the Kingdom to compromise their doctrines and their faith when confronted with the unrelenting pressure of conformity to the surrounding culture is timeless. From the Old Testament days of Barak and Baalam to the 1st Century days of Christians in Smyrna to the persecuted believers of Korea, the pressure to compromise our doctrine, our faith and our sexual purity is on-going. Those pressures to compromise

When Jesus Visits His Church

have only increased during the opening decades of the 21st Century as the biblical, Evangelical church has been challenged by our skeptical - even hostile - Postmodern culture on everything from the nature of the family to acceptable sexual behavior to doctrines such as Creationism, eternal punishment and much more. Add to this mix a growing political polarization over economic and social issues, and biblical Christians find themselves forced to examine their faith, their values and their obedience. We must ask ourselves what constitutes "faithfulness" to the Kingdom of God and what constitutes unbiblical compromise.

Compromise is a challenge and a threat to the Church of every age. Compromise comes in many forms, but in its simplest form, compromise manifests itself in "scandalous indifference" toward sin. For any believer to practice scandalous indifference toward sin is a personal affront to God's holiness, because it suggests that the God Whom we claim to worship is, Himself, indifferent to sin - which He is not!

Holiness simply defined is that attribute of God's nature whereby He is totally and completely separated from sin and is singularly devoted to His own glory. Because we do not appreciate the holiness of God, we do not fear Him in a genuine biblical sense. The people of Israel discovered both the holiness and the fear of God when they stood before God at the foot of Mount Horeb in Exodus 19. Isaiah rudely discovered this fear when he was confronted in the Temple by a vision of God in all His terrible holiness (Isaiah 6:ff). That

Epilogue

encounter with God's holiness transformed Isaiah. And in the process Isaiah discovered what David meant when he wrote under the inspiration of the Holy Spirit, *"The fear of the Lord is clean . . ."* (Psalm 19:9).

The New Testament Church in the Book of Acts was rudely introduced to God's holiness when He struck Ananias and Sapphira dead where they stood for the sin of intentionally lying to the Holy Spirit (see Acts Chapter 5) . The impact of that encounter with God's holiness upon the Church was profound: *"And great fear came upon the whole church, and upon all who heard of these things"* (Acts 5:11). God's holiness is not something to be trifled with. We worship and serve a holy God Who does not tolerate any compromise with or indifference toward sin.

The Biblical Antidote to Compromise

The biblical and time proven antidote to compromise is a personal and genuine encounter with God's holiness which re-instills a genuine "fear of God" and which produces genuine repentance and renewed intimacy with Him. This is the spiritual impact and legacy of those times of divine visitation when Jesus visits His Church, whether in the Book of Revelation, or in the book the Risen Christ is now writing about your house church. In contemporary terms we call such times of visitation times of "revival" or "spiritual awakening." Times of historic revival in the life of the Church have always been times when the Church of God rediscovers God's holiness and fear.

When Jesus Visits His Church

Earlier in this study, when we looked at the Church of Smyrna, we told the story of Christians in Korea and the persecution they experienced by their refusal to participate in religious ceremonies honoring the Japanese Emperor. What we didn't tell was the story of how the Risen Christ prepared the Church in Korea for those difficult times with a divine visitation, a season of revival and spiritual outpouring that re-introduced the Korean believers to the holiness and the fear of God, and poured into their lives the spiritual courage needed to face what would soon come upon the Church there. It was the visitation of the Risen Christ to the Church in Smyrna, again, only this time in Korea.

Smyrna In Korea

In November of 1904 a spiritual outpouring of historic proportions began in the small nation of Wales on the southwest coast of Great Britain. It quickly spread in every direction and by the winter of 1907 reports of its dramatic impact had reached the shores of Korea. In the winter of 1907, Presbyterian missionaries in Korea gathered with local believers for a week of Bible study and prayer. Graham Lee, an American, was leading a meeting of over 1,500 men. Before getting down to the business of Bible study he called for a brief season of prayer, and asked one man to open and another to close when two or three others had had the opportunity to pray. But by the time the first man had finished praying there were six more men standing and waiting to pray. When the second man finished praying there were a dozen more men standing to pray, and by the time the third

Epilogue

man had prayed, more than twenty men were standing to pray.

After several more men had prayed, Graham Lee interrupted and said, *"Well, apparently you want to pray. Alright then, instead of Bible study we'll have prayer. You may pray."* Immediately, all 1,500 men rose to their feet and began to pray. An eyewitness to the meeting said *"The effect was beyond description - not confusion, but a vast harmony of sound and spirit, like the noise of the surf in an ocean of prayer."* But along with the continued prayer came an intense conviction of sin as the holiness of God descended upon the gathering. An Englishman, Lord William Cecil, who was also present at these meetings, sent the following report to **The Times** of London, describing the scene:

." . . an elder arose and confessed a grudge against a missionary colleague and asked for forgiveness. The missionary stood to pray but reached only the address to Deity: 'Aboji!' 'Father!' when, with a rush, a power from without seemed to take hold of the meeting. The Europeans described its manifestations as terrifying. Nearly everyone present was seized with the most poignant sense of mental anguish; before each one, his sins seemed to be rising in condemnation of his life. Some were springing to their feet, and pleading for an opportunity to relieve their consciences by making their abasement known; and others were silent, but rent with agony, clenching their fists and striking their heads against the ground in the struggle to resist the Power that was forcing them painfully and agonizingly to confess

When Jesus Visits His Church

their misdeeds." [32]

God's holiness and fear seized the meeting, which was now beyond human control. Those events are best described by one of the missionaries who was there and was both a witness and a participant. What follows is William Newton Blair's account of that Tuesday night in January of 1907 when our God Whose Presence and holiness are "a consuming fire" came down and visited His people.

I wish to describe that Tuesday night meeting in my own words because part of what happened concerned me personally. We were aware that bad feeling existed between several of our church officers, especially between a Mr. Kang and a Mr. Kim. Mr. Kang confessed his hatred for Mr. Kim on Monday night, but Mr. Kim was silent. At our noon prayer-meeting Tuesday several of us agreed to pray for Mr. Kim. I was especially interested because Mr. Kang was my assistant in the North Pyengyang Church and Mr. Kim, an elder in the Central Church and one of the officers in the Young Men's Association of which I was chairman. As the meeting progressed, I could see Mr. Kim sitting with the elders back of the pulpit with his head down. Bowing where I sat I asked God to help him and looking up I saw him coming forward

Holding to the pulpit he made his confession. 'I have been

---

[32] J. Edwin Orr, ***Evangelical Awakenings In Eastern Asia*** (Minneapolis: Bethany Fellowship, Inc., 1975), page 28.

Epilogue

guilty of fighting against God. An elder in the church, I have been guilty of hating not only Kang You-moon, but Pang Moksa.' "Pang Moksa" was my Korean name. I never had a greater surprise in my life. To think that this man, my associate in the Men's Association, had been hating me without my knowing it. It seems that I had said something to him one day in the hurry of managing a school field day exercise which had given offense, and he had not been able to forgive me.

Turning to me he said, 'Can you forgive me? Can you pray for me?' I stood up and began to pray, "Aba-ge, Aba-ge," "Father, Father," and got no further. It seemed as if the roof was lifted from the building and the Spirit of God came down in a mighty avalanche of power upon us. I fell at Kim's side and wept and prayed as I had never prayed before. My last glimpse of the audience is photographed indelibly on my brain. Some threw themselves full length on the floor, hundreds stood with arms outstretched towards heaven. Every man forgot every other. Each was face to face with God. I can hear yet that fearful sound of hundreds of men pleading with God for mercy.

As soon as we were able, we missionaries gathered at the platform and consulted. 'What shall we do? If we let them go on this way some will go crazy.' Yet we dared not interfere. We had prayed to God for an outpouring of His Holy Spirit upon the people and it had come. Separating, we went down and tried to comfort the most distressed, pulling the agonized men to the floor and saying, 'Never mind, brother, if you have

When Jesus Visits His Church

sinned God will forgive you. Wait and an opportunity will be given to speak.'

Finally Dr. Lee started a hymn and quiet was restored during the singing. Then began a meeting the like of which I had never seen before, nor wish to see again unless in God's sight it is absolutely necessary. Every sin a human being can commit was publicly confessed that night. Pale and trembling with emotion, in agony of mind and body, guilty souls standing in the white light of that judgment, saw themselves as God saw them. Their sins rose up in all their vileness 'till shame and grief and self-loathing took complete possession. Pride was driven out; the face of man forgotten. Looking up to heaven, to Jesus whom they had betrayed, they smote themselves and cried out with bitter wailing, 'Lord, Lord, cast us not away forever.' Everything else was forgotten; nothing else mattered. The scorn of men, the penalty of the law, even death itself seemed of small consequence if only God forgave. We may have our theories of the desirability or undesirability of public confession of sin. I have had mine, but I know now that when the Spirit of God falls upon guilty souls there will be confession and no power on earth can stop it." [33]

The missionaries and Church leadership were horror-struck at some of the sins openly confessed, but all they could do

---

[33] *"The Korean Pentecost,"* excerpted from **Gold In Korea**, by William Newton Blair. Available through the Central Distributing Department of the Presbyterian Church (USA). 3rd edition (1957)

Epilogue

was watch the fire burn its way through the hearts of men who were now powerless to resist the workings of God's Spirit. It continued all that night, from eight in the evening until after midnight. Finally, at 2 o'clock in the morning, a lull gave the leadership an opportunity to pronounce a benediction and send everyone home. But the Risen Christ was not yet done with His Church. The same events took place the following night, only with greater intensity, and they continued nightly all week long, until the Holy Fire had burned its way through the Church and the body of Christ had been thoroughly cleansed by its encounter with the holiness and the fear of God.

In the meetings that followed, conviction of sin and reconciliation of enemies continued with deep confession of sin combined with restitution for past grievances. Non-Christian Koreans were astounded by what they saw, and a powerful wave of evangelism resulted. That terrible but wonderful meeting was, for all practical purposes, the birth of the contemporary Church in Korea. The Risen Christ had visited His Church, and by doing so He had prepared it for the tribulation and testing that would soon come upon it. In the words of William Newton Blair, who witnessed both the revival and the persecution, *"Christianity gives men backbone."* Yes it does. How does it do this? By instilling in them a vision of God's absolute and fearful holiness which causes them to walk in the genuine fear of their awesome God. He who fears God, fears no man. That spiritual truth is real whether you live in Smyrna or in Korea. And a man or woman filled with the holiness and the fear of God will not

When Jesus Visits His Church

tolerate scandalous indifference toward sin and will not quickly or easily compromise in the face of testing or tribulation.

Are You A Compromised Church?

The overarching message of the Risen Christ to the Seven Churches of Asia is a warning against the ever-present temptation of Churches to compromise with the world around them. So, the question must be asked, *"Are you a compromised Church?."* Has compromise with the world around you manifested itself in your life and in the life of your Church?

Are you shocked, and maybe a little irritated, that anyone would even ask you this question? Well, you probably aren't alone. I suspect that this message of compromise came as quite a shock to the unsuspecting believers of Asia Minor, and yet it was a genuine message regarding their true spiritual condition. That's the challenge during seasons of divine visitation and spiritual outpouring. During those times the Risen Christ reveals things to His people about their true spiritual condition that they were completely unaware of and that they don't really want to hear.

If you are feeling a little unsettled right now, perhaps it is because the Holy Spirit is speaking to you about things in your own life and the life of your Church that you need to deal with. Let me encourage you to pursue whatever He is showing you. And as you do so, let me remind you that the

Epilogue

most frequent command to the wayward believers of Asia is also the command of the Risen Christ to you: **Repent!**

A Prayer of Visitation

Heavenly Father, I seek your face in the name of Jesus of Nazareth, the Risen Christ, Who walks among the lampstands of your Church in great holiness and fear. I confess scandalous indifference toward sin and the compromises of my own heart. I repent of these and ask your forgiveness. I invite you to visit my life and my Church with your holiness and your fear. Show me those things to which I am blind and may not want to see, but which grieve your heart and need to be confronted and confessed. Grant me a spirit of repentance to respond with humility to the prompting of Your Spirit. Instill in me a backbone of spiritual courage fueled by your Holiness and fear and manifested through faith, love and good deeds. These things I ask in the name of the Risen Christ, and for His glory's sake. Amen!

"He who has an ear, let him hear what the Spirit says to the churches."

www.ingramcontent.com/pod-product-compliance
Lightning Source LLC
Chambersburg PA
CBHW070155100426
42743CB00013B/2912